Table of contents

Introduction

Light is one of the entities permanently present in our life. There is sunlight, moonlight, light from the stars; there is electric light, the light of the street lamps, the light of the fluorescent billboards. However, light is not merely a *natural* entity; it is not *inanimate* for us. All these objects have their influence on our psychics. The light of a candle, the light of a fireplace can make us remember a given moment or situation forever. There are many more phenomena related to light. It is so evident, so natural that light exists and is present in this world.

Still, this is not enough to define all dimensions of our understanding and perception of light. We do not think too much about it. We perceive it as something natural, as a part of nature. Of course, this is part of our, human, attitude toward the world: we perceive everything as natural, as real, as present all the time. This is the way in which our mind works. Moreover, light is really everywhere. It is a subject of philosophical discussions; of poetic works; of works of art. Light can be found in the Bible itself; in Plato's philosophical dialogues; in the poems of the greatest poets; in the paintings of Claude Monet; in the world's religions. All of us can understand what the poet- in this case, Whitman- has in mind while writing: "O SUN of real peace! O hastening light! /O free and extatic! O what I here, preparing, warble for!/ O the sun of the world will ascend, dazzling, and take his height- /and you too, O my Ideal, will surely ascend!" ("O Sun of Real Peace").

There are so many odes to sunlight; the sun is the symbol of life, of love, of peace, of happiness, of joy. It is not by accident that ancient tribes believed that the sun is a real god, that it is what maintains the order in the universe, that it is the creator of life. Light is life, light is good, light is what we need and should aspire to- this is what we are taught, what we feel, and what we realize.

On the other hand, there is darkness- the opposite of light. Darkness is associated with the long winter nights; with cold; with fear; with the dangerous. In pagan religions, evil gods are mostly connected with darkness. They are gods of the night, of darkness, of cold. The dark forest is a symbol of the realm of evil. Only in few cases darkness is perceived as something positive. Perhaps, only romanticism and other movements of the similar type have a positive attitude toward the dark. For romanticists, darkness means the unknowable, the mysterious, the power of the passions, the unconscious, the emotional side of human nature, and so forth.

Without any doubt, light and darkness are seen as connected, and even as mutually related. Dichotomies exist in unity, dialectics says (Heraclitus, Hegel). Light and darkness, thus, should be understood in their connectedness, in the fact that they are essentially related to each other. Such is the idea of Ancient Taoism, which saw the world as consisting of many dichotomical pairs- life and death, black and white, good and evil, light and darkness, Being and Nothing, etc., Taoism introduced the conception of Yin and Yang, two opposites which are always together. Chinese Taoism understood both as complementary elements which constitute the reality. As Ana-Teresa Tyminiecka observes: "Darkness without reference to light would have no degree in quality, no pitch, no intensity; in fact, it would have no qualitative endowment at all. This amounts to

saying that there would be no meaning of 'darkness.' And the same holds true for light"
(Tymieniecka VII). This is the approach which we can name *dialectical*. However, it is
not the only one: two more approaches can be elucidated. The *dualistic* approach will
analyze light and darkness are two co-eternal entities, or at least as the two central
constituents of this world. They are in an eternal struggle. This has its moral
consequences since human beings must take either of the sides. The *dominative* approach
takes it for granted that either of these powers is much stronger, and it is essentially
dominant. Most philosophers and religions see light as a dominating power, although
somehow connected with darkness. *Light is not to be understood as dependent upon
darkness. Light can be seen as an autonomous entity which can be better grasped by
contrasting it to darkness*, but *this does not mean that light has its origin in darkness*, or
that it is substantially related to darkness (as the first approach states). In the radical form,
this approach claims that *darkness is the absence of light* (Plato).

Now, *light has also another, spiritual dimension*. Light is often associated with
God, with the divine. Mysticism often refers to our *inner light*. Many religions in the
world refer to light as a manifestation of God. This conception is seriously taken even by
atheists. Even they cannot gainsay the fact that mystical experiences exist.

Regarding all this, our thesis runs as follows: God can be cognized both rationally
and in a non-rational way. *The rational way to cognize Him is strictly limited, but
mystical experiences can help us comprehend His essence without conceptualization*. The
Divine Light, the Light of God can be communicated to us through our own inner selves,
in situations which we call mystical experiences. The True Light of God is accessible in
such mystical experiences.

However, light is not associated only with mysticism. The philosophers of the Enlightenment (the very name of this period speaks a lot about its nature), for instance, identify light with the intellect. In the present book, we will also analyze such an approach, by discussing the function of our intellect and our consciousness, and their relation to the unconscious and the emotional side of our nature. It will be shown that light is often associated with consciousness, and vice versa.

There is one important emphasis in the present book. We will try to clarify the philosophical and theological dimensions of light. The reader will become acquainted with the idea that spiritual light is intrinsically connected with the good and with the divine. Light is thus the symbol of truth and the good at once.

In order to analyze our subject properly, the present book is divided into four sub-chapters. The first chapter deals with some mythological dimensions of the concept of light. Since the beginning of the history of humanity, light has always been interesting to human beings. It has been associated with divine powers. This is reflected mainly in the religions of Mithraism and Zoroastrianism. They take a dualistic approach and hold that the entities of Light and Darkness are co-eternal. What is interesting, Zoroastrianism also emphasizes on the concept of fire. We will try to answer the question: why is light so crucial for Mithraists? Why is fire one of the critical concepts in Zoroastrianism? To all this, we will add a short analysis of The Hinduist festival Diwali (festival of lights) and its spiritual meaning. An analysis of some passages of the book of *Genesis* will be carried out as well.

Having discussed the mythological understanding of light and darkness, we will proceed to its psychological dimensions. As we already remarked, some of our most remarkable memories are associated with light, fire, sunlight, and so forth. This concerns not only our sight but also other senses and perceptions. As many psychoanalysts have noticed, light has extraordinary effects on our psychics, and it can affect our behavior under given circumstances. The second chapter will turn to the way in which we perceive light and fire; to the psychological associations established during our encounters with these two entities. As it seems, sunlight and other sources of light have substantial influence on our psychics in early childhood, unlike other natural entities such as water, earth, air. Here we will turn to one philosopher and one psychoanalyst- Gaston Bachelard and Carl Jung. For Bachelard, fire is the meeting point of science and poetry. One can find in it a scientific concept, and a poetic concept as well. Carl Gustav Jung, on the other hand, states that light is consciousness. He analyzes the archetype of the Shadow- one of the psychological archetypes postulated by Jung. The Shadow is of negative essence; it always opposes the consciousness. The Shadow is also the unknown, what cannot be rationalized or understood.

This psychological and philosophical discussion will help us get closer to the essence of our topic: the nature of light seen in a metaphysical way. There are many experiences related to light which point to the reality of the divine. This will be the topic of the third chapter. Here we will turn to one Orthodox and one Catholic theory of Light as part of God's essence. We will ask the questions: Can we really see God? Is He visible? The majority of theologians say that God cannot be seen in all His glory; still, there are some ways to perceive Him. Here this problem will be discussed in the context of the debate on the nature of Tabor Light, a debate which appeared in the Byzantine Church in the 14th century. The question asked by the Byzantine theologians was: can

God's Glory, which appeared in the form of the Tabor Light (which is uncreated and is of divine essence), be really perceived? Alternatively, was this merely a natural light, having nothing to do with God? This discussion, although not taking place among Catholic theologians, can help us understand the essence of God as Light.

The concluding chapter of the present book will extend further the problem of light seen from a theological standpoint. Can light be the way to comprehend God's essence? Moreover, if the answer is affirmative, how can this be achieved? However strange, *mysticism offers the best way for communication with God*. This chapter, thus, will deal mostly with mysticism. *Illumination* is the most direct way to God, as it will be proved. People who have their souls illuminated can see and perceive God; they can communicate with Him. This is what we call mysticism. Three theologians will be discussed here: van Ruysbroeck, according to whom the Divine light is real, but it exists independently from God; Dionysius, who claims that God cannot be known positively but only by negation and/or analogy; and St. John of the Cross, who describes the spiritual journey of the soul to God.

As the reader will see, the central thesis of the book is based on the assumption that God exists in the way He is described by theologians. Theology, and particularly Christian theology will help us understand better the metaphysical properties of light. Evidently, light can be seen merely as a physical entity which cannot be subjected to theological analysis. Still, such an understanding will strictly limit our discussion on light. It will leave out the mythological and psychological dimensions of it, for example. It is clear that light and darkness are more than physical entities, more than natural processes. The Christian understanding will assist us in comprehending the reason why both concepts are consistently present in the world religions and mythologies, as well as in literature, art, and philosophy.

The scientific view of light will be omitted here, for we are to analyze light mainly from the standpoint of metaphysics and theology. Light is indeed an interesting issue in modern physics, and the research on it has led to the elaboration of Einstein's General theory of relativity, as well as to Quantum Physics, both being the two pillars of modern physics. Notably, the curious nature of light as being wave and particle at once (wave-particle duality) can be a subject (and has been such) of plenty of philosophical debates. Besides, we will not pay too much heed to the artistic perception of light. The majority of the most prominent artists in the world's history have elaborated their approach and use of light in their works. Such works of art will be referred to only in the context of our metaphysical analysis.

Chapter I: Mythology of light

The current chapter will begin our metaphysical analysis of light with some references to religions and mythologies which can be of use to achieve our goal. First, we will start with a short overview of the mythological dimensions of light. This will include a discussion on the conception present in the book of *Genesis*. Then we will turn to Mithraism and its dualistic approach to light and darkness. Finally, we will put to analysis Zoroastrianism with its dualism and particular emphasis on fire.

Why do we need to refer to mythology here? Because the first attempt to understand light as having transcendent status have its origin in ancient (more precisely-primitive) religions. As we will see, light had both symbolic and metaphysical value. It is part of religious ceremonies, and at the same time, it itself is deified, i.e., seen as divine in character.

1.1 Overview of the mythological concept of light

Summary:

This subchapter is a short introduction to the mythological dimensions of light and darkness. Several ideas related to them will be discussed, one of them being the Biblical concept of creation. Extreme and moderate dualism will be defined, and the moral symbolism of light will be discussed.

Ancient people perceived the world as consisting of various elementals. They believed that these elementals are of divine origin. Ancient people were not able to understand the way in which these elementals work. Fire, water, earth, air, and other elementals, were seen as extraordinary, as mystical, as not susceptible to any rational analysis. Light was essential for them since they knew that sight is our first source of information about the world. As Thomas Ryba remarks: "Perceptually, sight- light's associated sensory modality- is the most versatile; in comparison hearing, smell, touch, taste are all limited and more deceptive. Light enables sight to define a horizontal frame of reference which is centered on the physical individual" (Ryba 17). The function of light as providing us with information is pointed out as follows: "Light and sight thus provide a window on the world, a panorama, by which the whole is grasped" (Ryba 17). Other senses were also important, but they could not be compared with sight. This can be confirmed by language itself- we say "to see" not only when we mean our perception activity, but also when we want to say "to understand."

Without any doubt, the sun, the moon, and the other astronomical objects were perceived as gods, because their reality was completely incomprehensible for those human beings. The naïve intuition of the ancients helped them grasp the truth that the sun is vital for maintaining life on earth. They deified the sun, seeing it as intentionally giving light and heat to the world. The very fact that the geographic location of those ancient tribes and nations was not important (Nordic and Southern nations revered the sun equally) means that it is natural for human beings to understand the sun as one of the most critical physical objects whose existence we are aware of.

However, the geographic location could play some role in forming the mythological awareness of a given tribe or nation. One can distinguish Northern from Southern mentality. Here the name "Northern" refers to those parts of the world which experience long and harsh winter. Such tribes or nations naturally reflect more on the essence of night and darkness, on the function of fire and heat. For those living in the so-called South (meaning, the territories with an extended summer and mild winter, if there is winter at all), heat is something given; one does not need to work hard to produce it.

Celtic and Nordic (Scandinavian and German) mythologies are full of mysticism; darkness is very important for them. It symbolizes not only the lack of heat (and sunshine) but is a natural condition to which they adapt easily. This means, for the Northern mind darkness is not as a dramatic event as it is for the Southern mind. However, the very transition between day and night, light and darkness, has been subjected to many discursive and non-discursive reflections. As Sidney Feshbach writes: "Certain moments of light are impressionistic moments of processes that are given special privilege in myth and poetry, such as the mixtures for beginning's dawn and ending's dusk… that signify more than precise moments but entire attitudes" (Feshbach 58). There is a wide range of modes between absolute light and absolute darkness, and one can find exciting specifics of these modes. At any rate, there is some connection between light and darkness, as we will see in the fourth chapter of the present work.

Now, Greek and Roman mythologies did not pay heed to darkness; winter almost does not exist in these lands (with some exceptions). Thus ancient Greeks and Romans were convinced that heat and sunshine are *given* to them; that they are entirely *natural*. Nordic myths, on the other hand, claimed that light is purifying. The long night and harsh winter made these nations appreciate better the presence of sunlight and warmth. They

thus see light as something exceptional, an extraordinary entity. This should be kept in

mind by the reader- the mythologies which will be described in the following pages have

their specifics and are determined by the geographic, social and political context. At any

rate, for almost all world religions and mythologies sunlight is something to be preferred

over night and darkness.

Sunlight and light, in general, are postulated either as created in the very

beginning, or as having divine character. The latter option can be found in Ancient

Greece, Ancient Rome, in Nordic mythologies, in Ancient Egypt (where the supreme

deity was Amun-Ra, the sun-god), and others. Monotheistic religions, on the other hand,

claim that God created light. If we turn to the book of *Genesis*, we will find the following

passage about the creation of the world:

Now the earth was formless and empty,

darkness was over the surface of the

deep, and the Spirit of God was

hovering over the waters.

And God said, "Let there be light," and

there was light.

God saw that the light was good, and

he separated the light from the darkness.

God called the light "day," and the

darkness he called "night." And there

was evening, and there was morning the

first day (Gen. 1:2-5; *New International Version*).

The separation of light from darkness was the first act of God during the process of creation. This only demonstrates the importance of light. Light is good; light is truth; light is life. "God saw that the light was good," i.e., light is what the Creator planned and designed to create.

There is, still, another point to be mentioned: there are two types of light described in *Genesis*: primordial, and secondary light. Primordial light existed before the creation of the sun and the other astronomical objects. It means that in some sense it is another type of light, not the same which the sun radiates. Feshbach puts forth his interpretation as follows: "I see this light as primordial natural light, the alternative to which is not dark as such, but the prior chaos, chaos that at its thickest is primordial dark, and, later slightly less thick may be called wilderness" (Feshbach 61). In short, chaos was the opposite of primordial light. *Real darkness appeared after the creation of the astronomical objects*. The latter were created by God "to separate the day from the night", as it is written:

And God said, "Let there be lights in

the expanse of the sky to separate the

day from the night, and let them serve

as signs to mark seasons and days and

years,

and let them be lights in the expanse

of the sky to give light on the earth." And

it was so.

God made two great lights- the greater

light to govern the day and the lesser

light to govern the night. He also made

the stars.

God set them in the expanse of the

sky to give light on the earth,

to govern the day and the night, and to

separate light from darkness. And God

saw that it was good (Gen. 1:14-18).

Primordial light, thus, can be subjected to deep philosophical reflection. *Secondary light* is to be understood as strictly limited in the realm of physics. Primordial light is what philosophers have discussed in their works regarding the nature of the good, the reality, the truth, and so forth. As Feshbach asserts, primordial light is "the analogue, indeed, the phenomenological objective correlative, for certain kind of light intended in epistemological passages of the philosophers when writing about those mutual activities of 'presentation to the mind' and 'representation'" (Feshbach 62). What the author has in mind are texts by Plato, Plotinus, Descartes, and Husserl. Plato, for instance, used light as a symbol of truth in his allegory of the cave and the prisoners. Those who do not see the real sunlight, will think that it does not exist. But those that manage to escape from the cave will realize that there is real sunshine, and that it surpasses any possible light in the cave. Furthermore, light was seen by Plotinus as the symbol of truth. By contemplation, we can grasp the nature of reality, he claimed. Descartes, on the other hand, maintained that light is our intellect, and that when we use it properly, we will see everything in the right way; we will know the truth about the world. Edmund Husserl went further and asserted that there is a special process in which our consciousness can grasp the essence and Being of the world itself. This state of mind could be compared to Ancient Greek concept of contemplation. Hence, *primordial light is much more than physical light*: it is the symbol of reality, of Being, of the divine. This is the proper answer to the atheists that ask, how is it possible that God created light before the sun. *Atheists cannot comprehend the metaphysical dimensions of light.* As we will see in Third chapter, light can be also part of God's essence, and as being such, it cannot be compared to any material light, to the light which we see daily. As Feshbach observes: "We can suggest that the biblical primordial natural light, *ohr,* which is created before the secondary natural light, is analogous to a primordial mental light, *nous*" (Feshbach 68). This statement makes things clearer.

Light, as we stated already, was seen by Ancient people as having supreme status, as being more powerful than the other elementals. The relation day-night and light-darkness is, however, complicated among the so-called primitive religions. As it is pointed out in an encyclopedia article on the topic: "A wide-spread idea seems to be that night precedes or gives rise to day, darkness precedes or gives rise to light. Light, the light of day, appears to come gradually out of the darkness of night, whereas darkness falls over the light of day and extinguishes it" (Religion Facts sect. 1). This idea is also found in the quoted passage from *Genesis*: there was darkness at the beginning, and primordial light appeared as created by God. It can be explained by the fact that light and darkness are often seen as contrasting each other, therefore when light is absent, it must be dark. Day and light do not have their ontological origin in darkness but are rather preceded *chronologically* by darkness. *Darkness does not have the capability to create.* Light ontologically surpasses it: light is the higher entity. Light means life; it is awakening; it is joy and happiness: "Man also, asleep and inert during darkness, rises to fresh activity with the light. A pre-existing state of darkness, out of which light and life have proceeded, is thus usually presupposed" (Religion Facts sect. 1). This fact, we have to say once again, does not mean that the ontological cause of light is darkness. Likewise, the ontological cause of truth cannot be an untruth; evil cannot cause the good; and so forth.

Not all primitive religions held that darkness existed from the very beginning. Some dualistic conceptions asserted the opposite: "The Yezidis say that God made the world beautiful. Then Malik-Taus appeared before Him and said that there could be no light without darkness, no day without night, and accordingly He caused night to follow day" (Religion Facts sect. 3). As we will see in the next two sub-chapters, this is available in the Persian religions. This approach, which should be called dualistic, states that *light and darkness are equal in their might and that there is a constant struggle* between them. Darkness was created by the evil god as to oppose light, goodness, truth, and other attributes of the good god in these religions.

Some may claim that such dualism exists even in Nordic religions and mythologies. As it is remarked, "Grimm has suggested that many phrases in Teutonic languages used of light and darkness, day and night, show the one as a hostile, evil power in contrast to the kindly character of the other, and that there is perennial strife between the two" (Religion Facts sect. 7). At any rate, this dualism, if existing at all in Nordic mythologies, is not extreme. *Extreme dualism asserts that this struggle is eternal; moderate dualism claims that the Light and the Good will eventually prevail.* Nordic dualism, if it actually exists, does not go as far as Persian religions do. A possible explanation of Grimm's statement is that night and winter have a serious influence on the mentality and the way of living of Nordic people. This is the reason for darkness being perceived by them as having a permanent presence in their life.

Furthermore, we should not forget that coldness and darkness are often seen as interconnected, and even identical. Winter itself is comprehended as something to be avoided, as the only season of the year which is unpleasant and undesirable. This is especially true for the territories located near the North Pole, for night there is definitely shorter than day in some periods of the year. For instance, in Northern Norway, in Iceland, in Alaska, in Northern Canada there is a phenomenon called Midnight sun, which means that night itself is very short. Hence, the usual image of the North as experiencing long nights is not completely adequate. Winter is rather the concept which should be referred to here: in these countries/territories night is not long all the time, but winter is very long and usually harsh. Hence, winter and darkness could be used interchangeably. There is a severe deficit of heat during winter; hence, it can be easily identified with darkness, even though there is some sunlight.

The ethical dimension of light and darkness is not to be ignored. The primitive mind, it is said in the encyclopedia of religions, intuitively associates darkness with evil.

Gods related to darkness were perceived as evil, or at least not as good in their essence: "Evil gods, gods of death, etc., are often associated with darkness, or divinities who are not evil have often acquired a sinister aspect in so far as they are associated with the night or even with the moon, the ruler of the night" (Religion Facts sect. 6). There is no known case of a good deity related to darkness in the history of religions. In the best case, they are seen as mysterious (for instance, some lunar gods). Hence they should be avoided at any cost by common men[1].

Furthermore, darkness is understood as the realm of all magicians, wizards, and people of the kind. They do their activities in the dark and use the advantage that they cannot be seen. Darkness itself was perceived as having special energy which facilitates the magic "produced" by those magicians.

Darkness can also be comprehended as the *chronological* (not ontological) predecessor of light, as we already mentioned while commenting *Genesis*. It is not absolutely necessary to see light and darkness as opposed to each other. Some primitive mythologies grasp them as interacting with each other: "Since light, day, sun, seem to rise out of night, they are perhaps more often regarded as produced by darkness, rather than hostile to it, as in Polynesian mythology and elsewhere" (Religion Facts sect. 7). The ontological status of both is not to be seen as equal though. As Thomas Ryba observes: "Though light may be juxtaposed over-and-against darkness and may even presuppose darkness in order to be light; this does not mean that darkness necessarily has a similar status as an elemental form" (Ryba 18). Still, there is a diversity of opinions regarding a potential equality of light and darkness.

---

[1] Only special priests or magicians could deal with the influence of lunar gods.

Primitive mythologies are very diverse. It is hard to find a common principle which is universal and remains in the same form in each of them. Furthermore, we cannot have the whole information about all primitive religions and mythologies. However, from what we know by now, it can be concluded that *light and darkness are often identified with good and evil*, so they perform symbolic and moral functions. When myths speak about light and darkness, about the sun and the moon, about a Long Night or a Long Day[2], this should not be taken in its literal sense. These two concepts have a symbolic function; furthermore, they are essentially ethical. Light and darkness are always associated with moral categories in the context of mythology.

There is, of course, much more to add here. It is not by accident that hell was seen as a realm under the ground, as a dark place which is inhabited by shadows. We will analyze the understanding of the shadow in the next chapter, but now we can assert that the shadow represents a human personality, which is deprived of the fundament of its existence. The Shadow mean deprivation of life, of good, of individuality, of reality, and so forth. Ancient Greeks introduced the concept of *Hades*, which was their definition of hell. Hades is a dark place to which several rivers lead, and several rivers cross it. Ancient people, in general, imagined the area under the ground as completely dark and terrifying. It is far from sunshine; this means, Hades is far from any good, from any joy, from life. This conception is also encountered in Christianity, which perceives hell as darkness. However, there is one special difference: there is fire in hell, according to Christianity. The function of this fire, though, is not to illuminate the space; it should

---

[2] These concepts are often used in contemporary movies, for example *The Lord of the Rings* and *The Game of Thrones*. Extreme dualism is the basis of the plot: Light against Darkness (in the former movie), Fire against Ice (in the latter).

purify the souls of the unrighteous ones instead. It should also be remarked that Christianity generally does not perceive hell as a place on earth; hell is rather an immaterial, invisible reality. Still, the naivety of some ignorant believers has led them to think in terms of ancient Greek mythology: that hell is under the ground.

On the other hand, heaven, or the place where the souls of the righteous will feel joy, is depicted by many religions and mythologies as bright, full of sunshine. There is eternal day there; it is warm and bright all the time. Heaven is light itself, and true light is heaven. This has been and still is the way in which religions perceive heaven or places of a similar kind. This will be discussed in the third chapter.

Light and darkness can be seen as symbols in every field. Not only mythology and religion are their realm. As the Polish-American philosopher, Anna Teresa Tyminiecka observes: "The dialectic of light and darkness appears then… as the essential element in the poiesis[3] of life at large; playing in all its sectors: organic, vital, psychic, societal, spiritual and religious" (Tymieniecka VIII). It has multiple dimensions; it is placed in multiple realms- religion, ethics, art, science, and even politics. Any metaphysics of light needs to take this principle as its point of departure: light and darkness are universal concepts laden with plenty of meanings and connotations. As Tyminiecka adds, light and darkness are "the primogenital moments of the construction of this gigantic, existential sphere of the living being which perpetually glimmers in qualitative variety" (Tymieniecka VII). Wherever we direct our efforts to, whatever we do, we cannot exhaust these two concepts. *They are not simply words but are realities*

---

[3] An Ancient Greek word signifying creation, creativity.

themselves. This is the reason for narrowing down our analysis of light and darkness: to religion, metaphysics, and psychology.

Light and darkness, as we mentioned, are essential for understanding two central Persian religions- Mithraism and Zoroastrianism. Why are they so important for our analysis of light? Let us see.

1.2 Mithraism: the divine sun

Summary:

This sub-chapter offers a short discussion of Mithraism, and especially the associations of Mithra with the sun and light.

Two religions were most popular in the Roman empire in the first three centuries AD: Christianity and Mithraism. Roman paganism was slowly eliminated, and only noblemen adhered to it. Many things can be said about Christianity and how it was disseminated. The history of Mithraism is not less interesting. A religion having its origin in Persia, Mithraism is remarkable with the fact that it did not allow the Greek culture[4] to influence the religious environment in Persia.

On the contrary: Persian culture began its dissemination throughout the Roman Empire. Roman soldiers were interested in Mithraism. Of course, many more religions and cults penetrated the Empire, but this Persian-born religion was among the most important and influential.

---

[4] Although Rome had its own culture, it was seriously influenced by the Greeks, especially in the fields of art and philosophy.

The roots of Mithraism itself can be found in earlier pagan religions in the Middle East. As Feshbach remarks: "The Zoroastrian battles of Ahura-Mazda (or in descent, Spenta Mainyu) and Ahriman (or Angra Mainyu) refer to a cultural archetype that is found also in the earlier Sumerian stories of Gilgamesh and Humbaba, in Egyptian stories of Isis, Osiris, Anu, Mardu" (Feshbach 58). These "Zoroastrian battles" actually originate from Mithraism. This idea was perpetuated by other doctrines and religions, which would appear later in the form of "century-spanning thematic dualisms, such as Gnosticism, Manichaeism, and Kabbalism" (Feshbach 58). Therefore, Mithraism has various sources and various adherents.

It is hard to comprehend Mithraism as a homogenous teaching with one definite mental framework. Furthermore, it is claimed that Mithraism has something in common with the Vedic divinity of Mitra (who was the god of sunlight and heaven). As Feshbach remarks, there is also Assyrian and Egyptian influence on this Persian religion. Unfortunately, because this religion has not left too many traces, now we can rather make conjectures about its mythology. It is known that Mithraists believed in Ahura Mazda or the Creator of the world. Mithra was thus seen as a mediator between Ahura Mazda and mankind. His main task was to save men from the evil powers, which are led by Ahriman.

Two images of Mithra are universally known: Mithra as the sun, and Mithra as the bull-slayer. As one of the most prominent researchers of Mithraism, Franz Cumont, observes: "Mithra is the genius of celestial light. He appears before sunrise on the rocky summits of the mountains; during the day he traverses the wide firmament in his chariot drawn by four white horses, and when night falls he still illuminates with flickering glow" (Cumont 2-3). The symbol of the chariot is of primary significance: it indicates the function of Mithra as the one who maintains the cosmic order, the one who can provide humanity with support and help. Four was a magical number in Ancient times: it signified the four elementals, the four winds, the four directions of the world, and so forth. Mithra is in constant movement, and all the time he is the same. Mithra is in the sky, and Mithra is on earth. Mithra keeps the moral order in the world, and Mithra fights with the bull. There are many dichotomies found in the definition of Mithra as a divinity. Mithra is the sun, he is the light; he is thus happiness, life, and joy. As Cumont puts it: "The light that dissipates darkness restores happiness and life on earth; the heat that accompanies it fecundates nature… He is the dispenser not only of material blessings but of spiritual advantages as well" (Cumont 3). Mithra thus opposes the evil powers, which only want to do harm to all life and existence; to destroy all good in the world. His might is bigger than the power of the evil, particularly of Ahriman. Franz Cumont writes as follows: "The light that dissipates darkness restores happiness and life on earth; the heat that accompanies it fecundates nature… He is the dispenser not only of material blessings but of spiritual advantages as well" (Cumont 3). This is not the task of Ahura Mazda: he is simply the creator of the world. He sent Mithra to fight to evil and to maintain the order in the world.

This is a fascinating difference from Christianity. There is only one God in Christian theology. He is the source of light, of power, of strength, of life. There is no counterpart of Mithra in Christianity; this is the reason for our difficulties to understand his nature properly. Still, Mithra was seen by Ancient believers confessing Mithraism as their protector, as the one who can fight evil. For that reason, he was held to be the god of the warriors; and many Roman soldiers adhered to this cult.

Scholars comprehend Mithra's fight with the bull as an allegory of the suffering of man on earth. The bull itself symbolizes the problematic situations which we encounter daily. Moreover, still, there is something more in its essence: when Mithra slew the bull, all plants and animals in the world appeared out of the bull itself. In this sense, the act of murder was an act of creation as well. After this fight, the evil powers were awakened and decided to do anything to destroy life and all the good in the world. Mithra was victorious in this struggle, but we do not know if there was an ultimate battle between him and the evil. All that we know from the Ancient sources is that the struggle will continue for a long time. It is conducted in men's souls and the sky (between the stars, planets, and other astronomical objects, which were seen then as deities). Thus, Mithraism elaborated its own eschatology which we, unfortunately, do not know enough about.

Mithra himself helps human beings. As Cumont remarks, "Mithra was the 'mediator' between the unapproachable and unknowable god that reigned in the ethereal spheres and the human race that struggled and suffered here below" (Cumont 128). What is interesting, Mithra was not perceived as inhabiting heaven. Actually, it was believed that he inhabits a "middle zone," as Cumont points out: "For the ancient Magi[5], Mithra was… the god of light, and as the light is borne by the air he was thought to inhabit the Middle Zone between Heaven and Hell" (Cumont 127). This an interesting difference

---

[5] Magi were the followers of Zoroaster, who tried to reform Mithraism and founded Zoroastrianism.

between Christian God and Mithra: we cannot envisage a God Who does not inhabit heaven, but lives in the "middle zone" instead.

Another exciting aspect of Mithraism is its ethics. Ahura Mazda created the first human couple, and Mithra had to take care of them. The evil powers intended to capture them and to make them part of their forces. Only Mithra prevented this from happening, as Cumont observes: "It was in vain the spirit of Darkness invoked his pestilential scourges to destroy it; the god always knew how to balk his mortiferous designs" (Cumont 137). This is the ethical side of Mithraism: it makes sense of a world full of evil and suffering.

Mithraism could not omit the fundamental religion question- why is there evil on earth?-. The latter's answer includes *moderate dualism*- the good fights with the evil powers, and humanity is one of the "battlefields." We have, and we must to adhere to the moral principles of Mithraism, those people believed. In any other case, the war against the evil power (Ahriman) would be lost easily; man is thus one of the critical points of Mithraist worldview. By observing the given moral rules, believers will take their part in the eternal battle against Ahriman. If, on the contrary, some people decide to do whatever they want, and not to adhere to any moral regulations, then Ahriman will defeat the good without serious difficulties. Still, Mithraists believed that the battle's outcome has been already determined and that it is self-evident that Mithra will prevail for all eternity. Hence, the role of man in this cosmic battle is seen in a deterministic, fatalistic way: the good power has decided what to do with us, how to prevent us from sinning and wrongdoing. This should be contrasted with the Christian understanding of man's will: man is endowed with free will and his sins result from his own decisions. There is no fatalism in Christianity; God is understood as powerful, but giving the opportunity for man to decide what to do with his life.

The ultimate battle is to be fought in the future, as Mithraist eschatology teaches us. Ahriman was temporarily defeated by Mithra, but "the struggle between the good and the evil was still conducted on earth between the emissaries of the sovereign of Olympus and those of the Prince of Darkness; it raged in the celestial spheres… and it reverberated in the hearts of men" (Cumont 140). How will this battle be conducted and when? Who will take part in it? Are men also part of the battle? Will this be connected with the idea of Last Judgment? These are interesting questions which we cannot answer with certainty. All we know is that Mithraists believed that Mithra would say his last judgment, and he will decide who is a sinner, and who is righteous. However, when and where the final battle will take place, is not clear. Zoroaster, a follower, and reformer of Mithraism, attempted at elucidating this issue.

Before going to Zoroastrianism, we have to summarize the significance of Mithra and his relation to light. Mithra is perceived as the sun itself, and Mithra is light (in a spiritual sense). Interestingly enough, Mithra measured his strength with the sun and defeated it. He took the radiant crown of the sun on his head. Then he concluded a covenant of friendship with it, and they were allies (Cumont 132). Fire also had a specific role in Mithraism. There was a deity of fire: "Fire, personified in the name of Vulcan, was the most exalted of these natural forces, and it was worshipped in all its manifestations, whether it shone in the stars or in the lightning" (Cumont 114). The cult of fire would be emphasized later in Zoroastrianism. This connection is quite logical: fire brings light, and at the same time, fire purifies. Mithraism itself passed through different stages, especially when it was disseminated throughout the Roman Empire. Eventually, Mithraism was transformed- or there was the intention to do so- into a cult of one god only, Mithra himself. This is the assumption of Franz Cumont, according to whom around the 4th century AD, Mithraism was ready to establish a synthesis of various religious doctrines, by postulating the reality of only one god, the god of the sun, Mithra (Cumont 187-8). We cannot know what would have happened with this new cult had Christianity not been declared the official religion of the Roman Empire in the year 380 (the Edict of Thessalonica). At any rate, the role of light was important for Mithraism, and this idea would continue its existence in Zoroastrianism.

1.3 Zoroastrianism: light and fire

Summary:

Here the Zoroastrian practices and views related to fire and light are described. The role of fire is fundamentally vital in Zoroastrianism. Furthermore, this religion makes one step more toward ethical dualism, although this is due probably not to its founder but to later followers.

Unlike Mithraism, Zoroastrianism still has its followers. Because of this, we can have more information about its doctrine and practices. Furthermore, it has been suggested that the fundamental principles of Zoroastrianism have remained in the Manichean tradition, of which we know a lot thanks to the medieval Christian theologians.

It is not very known where to place the initial date of this religious doctrine. It is claimed that it appeared about three-thousand years ago. This makes it one of the oldest (if not the oldest) still practiced religions. The essential novelty introduced by Zoroaster was the *extreme dualism* of good and evil. This is the point for which he has been known (and criticized) for millennia. Still, as we will see further, the form of this dualism is still under discussion.

Zoroaster probably asked himself some questions regarding the nature of evil. This perhaps was the reason for reforming Mithraism and introducing the extreme dualism in his doctrine. Ahura Mazda created the whole world; therefore, evil things were also created by him. Zoroaster wanted to know, why should a good god create evil? He believed that this is not possible. Hence he decided to change some basic ideas of Mithraist ethics and cosmogony. This led him to dualism: the good god did not create the evil present in the world; it was instead created by the evil power, by *Angra Mainyu* (the spirit of evil). At the same time, the role of Mithra was relegated. Thus Ahura Mazda became the superior god in Zoroastrian pantheon. Ahura Mazda was seen as opposed to Angra Mainyu and the latter's army of *daevas*, or daemons. They started a battle, during which the evil forces destroyed humanity and all living beings, causing death and darkness to appear in the created world. This battle, which is to last for three-thousand years, requires the help of humanity, for only man is endowed with the opportunity to choose which side to follow. In such a way, Zoroaster does not deny the free will of man. The outcome of the battle is known, according to the Ancient prophet: Ahura Mazda and the army of the righteous will be victorious; the righteous will go to heaven, and the wicked ones- to hell.

The main principles of Zoroastrianism are recorded in the sacred book of this religion, *Zend-Avesta*. It contains original text written by Zoroaster himself (the so-called Yasna), as well as texts by his followers. It includes not only dogmatic principles but also rites and ceremonies. These texts have been probably changed and modified throughout the centuries, so we cannot be certain that we really read what Zoroaster himself wrote.

Two issues will be analyzed in the present sub-chapter: extreme dualism, and the function of fire and light in Zoroastrianism. We will not go too far in our exploration of this Ancient doctrine, for this will distract us from our task.

Extreme dualism is the idea *that there are two main gods, good and evil, who created, correspondingly, the good and evil things in the world*. Mithraism, according to our interpretation, adheres to *moderate dualism*. Zoroastrianism, on the other hand, goes further and claims that the battle between both sides is much more intensive and that the evil forces are equally powerful to their good counterparts. These gods, or as they are called in *Zend-Avesta*, primeval spirits, try to engage human beings on their side.

There are many passages in this sacred book that demonstrate Zoroastrian dualism. However, one can still ask: is Zoroastrianism really dualistic? There is one hypothesis according to which it is not extremely dualistic. Here we will turn to the conception of Douglas Fox. Fox observes as follows: "Zoroastrianism has popularly been represented as the classic example of a radical dualism that presents us with two gods: Ahura Mazda, who is good, and Angra Mainyu, the evil one (or Ohrmazd and Ahriman respectively" (Fox 129). He refers to the passage which postulates the reality of these two co-eternal principles (Yasna 30): "Now the two primal Spirits, who revealed themselves in vision as Twins, as the Better and the Bad in thought and word and action. . . . And when these twin Spirits came together in the beginning, they established Life and Not-Life" (quoted by Fox 130). Therefore, Life and Not-Life are the fundamental principles of Zoroastrian cosmogony.

As Fox explains: "All that comprises the world is the creation of one or the other of these two primal spirits, the good or positive elements ('Life') coming from one, and the evil or negative elements ('Not-Life') from the other" (Fox 130). This passage cannot be doubted, but there is another one which says something quite different. The author quotes a passage from Yasna 44 regarding the creation of the world, and comments that "There is here no attempt to divide the various parts of creation between two creators, and it is especially significant that light and darkness are attributed to the one creator, though darkness is commonly… the province and creation of Angra Mainy" (Fox 131). Darkness and evil are seen (in this passage) as a distortion of truth and light.

Furthermore, the battle between the two powers is not really eternal, it is rather temporary- and the victorious side is already known: "While Zarathustra sees the cosmos as a battlefield between good and evil forces, he clearly foresees a final triumph for Ahura Mazda and the good" (Fox 131). The battle will end, eventually, and then the good side will win. This is the basis of Zoroastrianism, according to this scholar. We can even perceive Zoroastrianism as monotheistic doctrine; he assumes: "There is a supreme creator who alone is God; but he has created two spirits, his sons, through whom the creation of the universe is effected. They, like God before them, have to choose Truth or the Lie, and each chooses differently" (Fox 133). The good and evil are, therefore, part of the act of creation. Ahura Mazda created them together. It cannot be known why; Fox himself is not able to explain it. At any rate, it is hard to claim that Zoroastrianism is monotheistic. This doctrine contains a whole pantheon- there are various gods in it. Mithraism in its late stage of development was closer to be labeled "monotheistic."

The reader may ask: why do we perceive Zoroastrianism as extreme dualistic doctrine, then? The answer offered by Douglas Fox is that the Magi distorted the initial doctrine of Zoroaster. As Fox asserts: "It is probable that the Magi added a number of innovations to Zoroastrianism. None was more significant than their clear-cut, rigid dualism in the concept of deity" (Fox 133). Hence, the Zoroastrian doctrine has not remained in its original form. It has been changed, and perhaps this has occurred many times. The motivation behind the change conducted by the Magi was the one mentioned earlier in this sub-chapter: that the supreme god cannot be the creator of all evil. The Magi, Fox writes, "were unable to accept the implication that the good God could have had any part, even indirectly, in the creation of that which is evil. They thought they were defending his integrity by separating him radically from the source of all that opposed his honor" (Fox 134). In short, not Zoroastrianism is dualistic; the changes done by the Magi are dualistic. In this form, Mani and his followers- the Manicheans, borrowed some ideas of Zoroastrianism.

What difference does this make regarding our understanding of light, then? Extreme dualism asserts that the good and evil powers are co-eternal and equal in might. This means light and darkness should also be comprehended as co-eternal. Therefore, darkness is eternal in its essence. On the other hand, moderate dualism and monism claim the opposite- that darkness is only *temporary*. Monism even goes further and says that darkness is the absence of light. Hence, the hypothesis that Zoroastrianism was not dualistic from the very beginning can influence our understanding of the Zoroastrian view of light.

Light is perceived by Zoroastrians not merely as a physical entity. Light and fire have a special place in Zoroastrian mythology and rituals. Here we will refer to an article by K.E. Eduljee, a scholar researching all aspects of Zoroastrianism. He has collected only the most critical points of significance related to the use of fire and light in Zoroastrianism. Before describing the Zoroastrian view, Eduljee turns to the fundamental role of fire in humanity's life. It can be said, he asserts, that the discovery of fire established the first human civilization[6]. As he remarks: "The ability to make, build and ignite fire was undoubtedly the single most important discovery that enabled the civilization of human beings. By learning to use fire, people gained a decisive advantage over all other species" (Eduljee par. 4). The outcomes of this discovery, however strange this seems to us nowadays, were very important in the past: "Fire made it possible for people to populate land in the colder regions of the earth. Fire produced light and provided protection. Fire enabled food to be cooked and for human beings to benefit from a wide range of nutrients" (Eduljee par. 4). In short, fire was so crucial for primitive people that they used it in their religious practices, and there was a place for it in their system of religious beliefs.

Of course, today we still do not know too much about the religions of pre-Ancient people. At any rate, light, fire, and the sun were among their deities, and were related to their rituals. Zoroastrianism, as the descendant of the Ancient Iranian religion (thus, indirectly- of the Vedic religion in what is today India), has thus preserved the cult

---

[6] From standpoint of evolutionism, which holds that primitive man discovered fire all of a sudden.

of fire and light. Fire is used in Zoroastrian practices; it is a crucial concept in Zoroastrian mythology. Fire is the necessary element which has to be present in Zoroastrian temples. Fire is associated with Zoroastrian burial ceremonies. Fire is created by the supreme god himself, by Ahura Mazda. However, what else can be said about fire in Zoroastrianism? As it seems, it has more meanings than the ones we usually think of. Fire is always present in Zoroastrian temples, Eduljee observes and explains that fire symbolizes wisdom and truth: "Carrying a fire into a dark place dispels the darkness giving us the metaphor of the light of wisdom banishing the darkness of ignorance. From wisdom are derived the principles of justice and order" (Eduljee par. 2). Material fire, or fire which we can see, touch, smell, and so forth, is not divine itself; but it points to fire as a divine entity: "The temporal fire was also the symbol of the cosmic fire of creation, a fire that continues to pervade every element of creation. In this sense, fire takes on a much broader meaning than a flame" (Eduljee par. 2).

To prove that fire has a special place in Zoroastrianism, the author refers to five types of fire which are as follows: (1) in inorganic materials; (2) in the human and animal bodies; (3) in plants; (4) in the clouds (lightning); (5) and in a flame (temporal fire) (Eduljee par. 6). These types of fire were part of the cosmic fire of creation. Furthermore, Zoroastrianism conceives fire also as energy. Energy is to be associated with power, with might. Hence, fire was created by the mighty god, and not by the evil. This fact itself speaks against the theory that good and evil are equal. No, they are not equal: the good is much stronger, and it has the true power on its side. Darkness is not equal to fire, to light; darkness is much weaker, and fire can always dissipate it. As Eduljee observes: "The fire or energy of creation… is a direct creation of God, Ahura Mazda, and that the material universe… coalesced from the 'fire' or energy of creation" (Eduljee par. 12). As a creation of god, fire is endowed with all divine attributes, such as truth, reality, wisdom, power, and so forth. Truth is called by Zoroastrians *asha*. *Asha* is fire, and fire is *asha*: "In the Avesta, fire as the cosmic fire of creation is intimately connected with asha, the cosmic laws through which order in the universe is maintained. The temporal fire is seen as a symbol of asha" (Eduljee par. 10). The fire is true, and everything true is fire.

Fire maintains the cosmic order, in the same way in which Mithra does it, according to the teaching of Mithraism. Fire is truth because it helps one understand the essence of reality. This adds another dimension to the metaphysical understanding of light- truth, and veracity. Light helps us see the world correctly. When it is dark outside, we are not able to see anything as it is in reality. Material fire, of course, is not the truth itself; it is a symbol. When the believer practices the rituals of Zoroastrianism, he is always aware of the presence of fire, of light, of energy in his earthly life; this symbolic fire should remind of the eternal truth, of the reality which stands beyond our normal understanding of the world. As Eduljee explains: "At the heart of a Zoroastrian place of worship burns a fire- traditionally a wood fire- and where possible the fire burns continuously symbolizing an eternal flame with all the attendant meaning we have discussed above" (Eduljee par. 16).

However, fire is not merely the objective reality; since fire is truth itself, it can also be found in our hearts, in our souls. Here comes the specific role of humanity. We have to adhere to the truth, to the righteous way, as Eduljee remarks: "Zarathushtra makes reference to the mainyu athra - the spiritual fire - as one that illuminates the path of asha. The universal laws of asha govern and bring order to the spiritual and material existences" (Eduljee par. 13). Asha still does not determine our moral conduct; we have the choice to decide which side to take. Asha or the truth (wisdom, order) will guide us through the process: "Asha is available, through individual choice, to bring order to human thoughts, words and deeds" (Eduljee par. 13). Good thought, good word, and good deed are the three noble principles of Zoroastrianism. Thought, word, and deed are always connected and interdependent. When we have found ourselves on the right way, our thoughts and deeds will be the right ones. *We have the chance to take part in the universal battle and to help the good power to defeat the enemy.* This is the ethical side of Zoroastrianism.

1.4 Fire in other religious practices

Summary:

Three cases of practices with the use of fire will be discussed in short here: eternal flame, midsummer bonfires, and the festival of Diwali. This will allow us to find more meanings in the use of fire in religious practices.

Zoroastrianism is only one among the many religions that puts emphasis on fire. Practices involving the use of fire are not uncommon among human beings, whatever their culture, geographic location or religion are. There are three more phenomena, which we can refer to in the current chapter: eternal flame; the Indian fest of Diwali; and the pagan ritual of midsummer with its bonfires.

Eternal flame is so popular nowadays, it is so universal, that we think of it as something usual. There are dozens of eternal flames in this country, and all we know what they symbolize. Eternal flame is an act of remembrance. It is present at war memorials all over the world. It is assumed that this flame burns for an indefinite time, which means, we cannot know when it will extinguish. However, eternal flame is not a product of modernity. It appeared in ancient times: in Greece, Egypt, among Zoroastrians, among Israelites. Probably it was also used in other Ancient societies and religions. In Greece, the flame originates from the Olympic tradition, which showed its reverence to the goddess Hestia. The Olympic flame meant for Greeks that the gods protected them, it was their indirect connection with the gods.

Furthermore, it had some associations with Prometheus, who, according to the myths, took it from Zeus and gave it to human beings. Today, eternal flame does not have anything to do with the gods. It refers rather to the memory of those who have fallen in certain wars, or in defense of their fatherland. Without a doubt, it is of symbolic nature.

Nevertheless, when one stares at the fire and thinks about the fallen ones, one cannot but see more truths about life, about the meaning of life, about the difficulties which we encounter in our earthly existence. Eternal flame, in short, has an influence on our thoughts and worldview. This is a practice which we have taken as usual, and it is rare that someone asks what its roots are. Its roots are spiritual and religious: the eternal flame is silent; it does not show anything, but it shows enough, it speaks enough. When we open our eyes and our mind, we will understand that it points to another, ultimate reality; that it says to us: "Earthly existence is short, but there is another reality where one can live forever."

Religious practices in Ancient times were not based only on fire and sunlight, of course. There were other essential elementals used, such as water (as in Christian Holy

Baptism). Fire has been, still, very important for many national and ethnic traditions.

There has been one pagan tradition, which has survived for thousands of years, and it

unites at least half of the European nations as well as their descendants in North America

and Latin America: midsummer. Midsummer, of course, is not the only European festival

with use of fire. However, it is probably the universal one- it has been practiced in Spain,

Italy, Germany, France, Scandinavian countries, Slavic countries, Ireland, in some parts

of the United Kingdom. The emigrants from these countries introduced the same

practices to the United States, Canada, Mexico, Brazil, and so forth.

Midsummer, or the St. John's Eve, celebrates a very important astronomical

event: solar solstice, or the longest day after which the day duration slowly decreases.

Midsummer was a completely pagan practice, but it was not possible for the Church to

eradicate it. It was later re-introduced as the St. John's Eve in memory of St. John

Baptist[7]. As James Frazer observes in his remarkable study of religious ideas, *The Golden

Bough*: "All over Europe the peasants have been accustomed from time immemorial to

kindle bonfires on certain days of the year, and to dance round or leap over them" (Frazer

535b). The importance of the celebration was related to the astronomical event which

occurs only once yearly: "The summer solstice, or Midsummer Day, is the great turning-

point in the sun's career, when, after climbing higher and higher day by day in the sky,

the luminary stops and thenceforth retraces his steps down the heavenly road" (Frazer

546b). Midsummer has been celebrated with bonfires. People usually jump over the

bonfire, or dance and sing around it. Sometimes they burn effigies, or even live animals.

---

[7] This practice is still mainly of pagan nature.

Why is fire chosen for such a celebration? The participants will say that fire keeps them from evil spirits, and fire also cleans and purifies. This holds true as of human beings, animals, and plants. Human beings will be healthy and strong; the house stock will survive; all diseases will stay away; crops will be fertile; and so on. As Frazer explains: "The fire is believed to promote the growth of the crops and the welfare of man and beast, either positively by stimulating them, or negatively by averting the dangers and calamities which threaten them" (Frazer 564a). The general explanation of the practice is that fire cleans and protects. This is probably so not only because of the properties of fire itself but also because fire resembles the sun. Sun, as it was believed in pagan times, can influence the course of events on earth. It can protect from diseases, from various calamities. Pagans believed that by imitating the sun, they would receive its "mercy" and help.

The protection of men, animals, and plants from evil spirits was important, as we remarked. According to Frazer, fire (as symbolizing the might of the sun) was perceived as protection. For example, in the case with the belief that bonfires will increase the fertility of human beings (it will help the childless families), "this happy effect need not flow directly from any quickening or fertilising energy in the fire; it may follow indirectly from the power of the fire to remove those obstacles which the spells of witches and wizards notoriously present to the union of man and wife" (Frazer 571a). It should be noted that similar rituals take place in winter, and in some parts of Europe- at the end of April (the so-called Walpurgis night). Winter is often seen as the time of the year when evil spirits have much power to attack people and animals. There is a difference between them, though: midsummer bonfires are related instead to fertility, and winter bonfires are produced by the belief that the dark powers (the evil spirits) are very powerful, and people must protect themselves.

Finally, there should not be any doubt that bonfires symbolize the power of light in general. As Frazer points out: "At the festivals which we are considering the custom of kindling bonfires is commonly associated with a custom of carrying lighted torches about the fields, the orchards, the pastures, the flocks and the herds" (Frazer 568a). He adds that "we can hardly doubt that the two customs are only two different ways of attaining the same object, namely, the benefits which are believed to flow from the fire" (Frazer 568a). The object is the power of light, which can cleanse, purify, protect, empower, and so forth.

Dances, songs, and other rituals accompany the main ritual- jumping over the bonfire. These dances and songs are part of folklore traditions that aim at forming and sharing a collective memory. It is not surprising to see that midsummer can be found even in North Africa (as Frazer asserts). However, festivals of lights can be found in Asia as well. One of the most interesting of them is the Indian festival of Diwali. Diwali is among the most popular Indian holidays which is celebrated worldwide by the Indian communities (as well as other people from neighboring countries). It is part of the Hinduist tradition (not to be confused with Buddhism). *Diwali is centered on the concept of light.* People gather together to celebrate. As it is described on the website Diwali festival, "they give expression to their happiness by lighting earthen 'diyas' (lamps), decorating the houses, bursting firecrackers and inviting near and dear ones to their households for partaking in a sumptuous feast" (Diwali par. 1). If one asks why exactly lamps and candles are used, the answer is as follows: "The lighting of lamps is a way of paying obeisance to god for attainment of health, wealth, knowledge, peace, valor and fame" (Diwali par. 1). Usually, people pray to Lakshmi, the goddess of happiness and wealth. Light itself symbolizes the good, the truth about the world, as well as wisdom and knowledge: "To Hindus, darkness represents ignorance, and light is a metaphor for knowledge" (Diwali par. 4).

Wisdom and knowledge are very important for the Hinduism tradition. The *Vedas* (the most ancient Hunduist sacred books) speak of the true knowledge of the world. According to them, the world exists in unity, and the existence of individual beings (especially- human beings) is a product of an illusion. We perceive our Ego as really existing; and this, according to the Vedas, is wrong. This illusion makes us want to gain various material and immaterial things. In such a way, we become attached to the world, and this itself leads to an endless cycle of reincarnations. Only true knowledge can help us get rid of this illusion, and thus we will be able to stop the cycle of reincarnations. Thus, light symbolizes this knowledge: that the world is one whole, and that individual souls are part of a vast, universal soul- Brahman. This festival reflects the belief that man will become able to stop all these reincarnations, and will unite himself with Brahman. As it is remarked, "Lighting a lamp symbolizes the destruction, through knowledge, of all negative forces- wickedness, violence, lust, anger, envy, greed, bigotry, fear, injustice, oppression and suffering, etc." (Diwali par. 4). All these vices are rooted in the illusion that the Ego (Atman) is real, and that it is different from all other souls (Egos).

We can finally ask, what are the essential differences between the Zoroastrian view of fire, the bonfires of Midsummer, and Diwali. In all three cases, fire means light; but in Zoroastrianism, it points to another reality which surpasses this world. God, who created the world, is light himself; and light is good. In Diwali, light points to wisdom and true knowledge (about the identity of Atman and Brahman). Midsummer's bonfires, in turn, serve as protection against the evil power; this protection is based on the belief that bonfires imitate the sun and with their light, they can drive out any evil spirit. *Ergo*, there are some specifics of each form of religious practice involving the use of fire and light. There can be more examples to be exposed here: festivals related to light and fire are found everywhere, but their essence is similar.

1.5 Conclusion

The current chapter has shown various mythological and religious dimensions of the concept of light. As one of the elementals, light has always been used in religious practices; there have been many mythological ideas connected with light. Light has signified the good, the true knowledge, the ultimate reality, and also other notions such as immortality, divine reality, wisdom, etc. Therefore, light has metaphysical nature, and we should not conceive it only as a physical phenomenon.

From mythological aspects of light, we can easily go to its psychological dimensions, since, mythology and human psychology are related to each other. What can be said about the human perception of light? Is light important for human beings from a mental standpoint? We will try to find the answer in the following chapter.

Chapter II: Psychological aspects of light

As an important entity, process and phenomenon, light influences our memories, reactions, and views. This includes all forms of light: sunlight, artificial light, fire, candlelight, neon billboards, moonlight and light from the stars, and so forth. Light appears in our dreams; light is depicted in many paintings; light makes it possible for us to take pictures and to shoot videos. We cannot imagine a world without any light. As Sidney Feshbach puts it: "Everyday light, everynight dark; daylight: sunlight, brilliant and varying, shadows, the edges of light and shadows, sharp and fuzzy; nightlight; moonlight and moon in phases of changing" (Feshbach 57). These are the sources of natural light. But there is light produced by human beings, and among them we find nuclear explosions: "There are those terrible images in the photographs of nuclear explosions and the sidewalks in Hiroshima bleached so intensely that, seemingly, people left their shadows burned into the surface" (Feshbach 57). There are so many examples of light- pleasant, joyful, terrible, disastrous!

Speaking about psychological dimensions of light, what should they include? Psychology is, of course, connected with religion, ethics, with the society, with politics. There are no dimensions of light which are completely and absolutely psychological and do not belong to any other sphere. For example, the feeling of pleasure when we stand in front of a fireplace on a cold night is psychological; but it can also be used in mythology. The moonlight is very romantic, but its analysis can belong not only to psychology but to art as well- moonlight has been depicted in many brilliant paintings, in many exquisite poems. What we consider being psychological aspects of light in our life are various impressions, emotions, feelings, memories, associated with light. If the reader object that these aspects are not so important, we can turn to examples such as: the memory of the first experience with candlelight in the darkness; a romantic walk under the starry sky and the full moon; the craving to go to a distant, exotic place with a lot of sunshine and opportunities for relaxation; and so forth.

Evidently, the psychological dimensions of light are not only positive. One can be afraid of sunburn, or have a bad experience with heat, or one can have a memory of his/her first touch of the flames of a bonfire. Our feelings and emotions are not always good and pleasant. To all this, we will add the perception of darkness. One of our basic fears, as some psychoanalysts claim, is related to darkness. Darkness is a phenomenon which we cannot avoid, and this makes it so exciting and important. Darkness is not perceived as bad in itself by human beings; this is so because we have been used to living in the dark- especially our predecessors in the pre-industrial era when there was no electricity but only candlelight.

This is only the general framework of the chapter. Let us begin our analysis now. The current chapter will first present the views of the philosopher Bachelard regarding fire and light, and then we will turn to Carl Jung's theory of the archetype of the Shadow as the unconscious part of our personality. This will help us understand more about the metaphysical dimensions of light.

2.1 The perception of light: some remarks

Summary:

Here some issues related to perception will be discussed in short. Analysis of our fear of the dark will be carried out, as a preparation for the second sub-chapter.

Light plays a much more critical role in our life than we usually think. We already mentioned in how many situations we can have experiences related to or including light. What is even more interesting, is the fact that the human organism is subjected to the influence of light. Light, as scientists have shown, influence the processes running in our bodies. Still, it exerts also influence our psychical processes, so it should not be reduced to a purely physical phenomenon.

Without a doubt, the perception of light is connected with our perception of the world around us. Cognitive psychology has demonstrated that the perceptive process takes place in our brain, and not in the senses. One century ago, some psychologists believed that our perceptions are formed independently from the brain, and the brain only conceptualizes them. When I see a red apple, my senses gather the information about the apple and then pass it to my brain. The image, taste, and other sensible qualities of the apple are already formed, and our brain only puts the label with the name "red apple" on them. This was the train of thought also of some philosophers of the 18th and 19th century, especially the British empiricists (John Locke, David Hume, and others). Light, according to this theory, should be comprehended as an independent entity, i.e., separated from all material objects.

This turned out to be wrong. As cognitive psychology in the second half of the 20th century has shown, this is not the case with human perception. We perceive the world as one whole, and we do not perceive all objects separately from each other. I perceive the red apple as a whole; I do not perceive the color "red," the object "apple," and the taste of an "apple" separately. All these perceptions form one whole from the very beginning. This is due to our brain activity: our brain "recognizes" the red apple, and then the senses add more and more information to this already formed perception. We will not go into details here, but it suffices to say that the existence of optical illusions prove the veracity of the "top-bottom" theory, or the theory that our perceptions (the "bottom") are formed in the brain (the "top"), and not in our sense receptors.

Nonetheless, light does not affect only our perceptions, as Rosella Tomassoni and her team of researchers assert: "Light was analyzed not only by a perceptive point of view, but also as a driver of cognitive, emotional and behavioural responses by the perceiver in different experiential contexts of everyday life" (Tomassoni et al. 1216). As it seems, our behavior is affected by light: "It showed that light is a Cognitive Map able to guide and direct the individual in the exploration and discovery of the surrounding environment, providing the interpretative keys of an increasingly complex reality" (Tomassoni et al. 1216). This means we need light to adapt ourselves to a certain environment.

For example, if it is dark outside and we stroll around the streets of a city which we visit for the first time, we would be perplexed. Perhaps this will also lead to distress and psychical tension within us. This is only a simple example. Light is used especially at work: whether it is sunlight or electrical light, it keeps us awake and maintains our concentration. It is hard to imagine office work in a dark room. Electrical light itself is not so appropriate for work, but sometimes people are forced to use it because there is no sunlight (or natural sources of light). When we want to sleep, on the other hand, light is what can disturb us. It is advisable to have less light in the room where we want to sleep. Any sources of light, including artificial ones, are obstacles to our sleep. There are many more things to say here: that the color of the light can also orientate us where we are right now (fluorescent billboards will tell us that we are somewhere in the center of a big city, for instance); it can advise us what to do, how to behave (the flashing lights in the disco club affect the behavior of the attendees); the brightness of the light is important (as in the case with the office work); any change of light can also have some influence (it can be irritating); the lack of change itself can be irritating (during police interrogation, constant and non-changing light is used to make the suspected person more nervous and to confess more things); and so forth. As Tomassoni and her team remark: "Over-lighting or close light flashes provoke dazzle, that by reducing the perceiver's visibility and visual performance, bring out discomfort, stress… in the individual, that if sustained over time may lead to neuropsychiatric disorders" (Tomassoni et al. 1220).

Light is also used in architecture and design. Architects have to manage with all challenges related to light and lighting. People want to live in comfortable homes, therefore it is essential for the architect to prepare such a design which will allow the building (or premise) to have access to natural light. The latter itself also means the possibility to heat the premise in a natural way (instead of using other methods for heating such as gas or electricity). Bright rooms are preferred for living by most people; dark rooms are used for storing unneeded stuff.

Given that we need light to orientate ourselves in the world (as was mentioned above), it is of primary importance to know what time it is right now; whether it is day or night; what is the weather outside (again, this is related to our perception of light- when it is dark in the day, it means there will be a storm or another unpleasant occurrence). Scientists have found that our body adheres to a certain bio cycle, thanks to which we are ready to sleep at night, and we are prepared to work during the day. Light has some connection with this cycle, as the researchers observe: "Human life is marked by the alternation of night/day, dark/light, sleep/wake and work/rest rhythms" (Tomassoni et al. 1219). For instance, they add, "light influences biochemical and hormonal processes, body temperature, mood, psychological well-being and electrical brain activity, influencing the neurotransmitters" (Tomassoni et al. 1219). Light thus triggers processes which are important for staying awake, or for being able to sleep. This is a fact which has been explored recently, and it only confirms the veracity of the cognitive theory about the relation sense-perception. Philosophers, artists and writers in the past were not able to understand the fact that we do not merely perceive light, but light itself affects our physiology, it leads to changes in our behavior, and can even influence our emotions. Our mood can change due to light. For instance, when we travel from a cold place to a sunny and warm place (for example, during winter), we feel better and have a more positive attitude; and the other way round: when we visit a cold place for a while, our mood is affected negatively. We feel something of the type of depression or melancholy. This is due to both heat and light; but without sunlight, there would not have been any heat, so they both are connected.

Christmas decorations are another example. Why are there so many electrical lights for Christmas? Not only because lights symbolize God and the birth of Jesus. During the dark and cold winter, artificial lights can improve our mood, and thus help us celebrate with more enthusiasm. Not to forget the very fact that the Christmas tree, which shines brightly at home, creates long-lasting memories. We all remember the Christmas tree from our childhood and associate it with warmth and the care of our parents. The color of the lights and the composition of the decoration is unique, and at the same time universal- all Christmas decoration resemble each other because human beings have the same perception of light.

As we see from the examples given above, the researchers claim, "Light is, therefore, a device (natural or artificial) that supports the brainwork of reconstruction and classification of reality by the viewer, setting the syntax rules of visual perception" (Tomassoni et al. 1218). It is high time we stopped thinking of light only as a physical phenomenon and began comprehending it as a whole set of connections, associations, influences, and so forth. We have to listen to the voice of science if we want to understand better the nature of light. As Tomassoni and her team remark: "Light has not only the role to make *visible* an object for a viewer, but also to contextualize it within the environmental space" (Tomassoni et al. 1218). Light is one of our main guidelines which help us orientate and adjust ourselves. Other of them are heat, water, air- elements, which we need and without which we could not survive. At any rate, of all them, light has the most significant metaphysical potential. It involves many meanings, perceptions, emotions; it influences both our body and mind; and finally, light is found in the material objects, so it is not entirely independent. Of course, all this is said from the scientific point of view, i.e., the view that light is mainly physical phenomenon.

Our well-being, our positive attitude toward life also depends on light and lighting (to which we should add heat). Light stimulates our organism and triggers processes which can ensue in our better mood, in our better ability to work, in our preparedness to sleep normally and calmly, and so forth. Psychologically, light is what can influence positively: "This specific type of stimulus is able to excite, move, impress, communicate, heal and generate wellness, creating a sense of harmony and syntony with the surrounding environment" (Tomassoni et al. 1217). On the contrary, darkness affects us negatively: "The *dark*, namely absence of light, contributes to organize and set out the surrounding environment, marking emptiness and fullness, presence and absence" (Tomassoni et al. 1218). In this sense, darkness can also orientate us in the world: the same which we said about light, can also be attributed to darkness, but in the opposite direction.

What is darkness, from a psychological standpoint? All we have some experience of being the dark. The first word which comes to our mind is "fear." Yes, we feel fear; and especially children have a strong fear of the dark. Another word is "unknown." Darkness symbolizes what is unknown, what is strange, what is incognizable. We naturally tend to avoid the dark, except some romantic moments. Romantic persons themselves use the power of the dark to suppress their intellect and to get rid of their prejudices and preliminary plans. *Our emotions are stronger in the dark.*

Where does the fear of the dark come from? What is its origin? It can be assumed that it is related to our physiology, which, as we have seen, is essentially influenced by the presence/absence of light. Light and heat make us feel more comfortable, more convinced, more relaxed, more energetic (depending on the situation). Their absence ensues in the feeling of insecurity, in worry. This is natural, on the one hand; on the other hand, it can be based on our life experiences. We are taught (socially, not in school) that it is better not to walk alone in the dark, that it is good to have some light near to you when you are at home, and it is dark outside, etc. According to Vamshi Krishna, who summarizes in simple words the theories of the psychologists regarding the dark, the explanation can be the following: "As we hear/study about the crimes and acts of violence happening at night our minds become more scared of the dark. This is the reason still most of us are a bit afraid of the dark" (Krishna par. 4). Reading books, watching movies, hearing the news about such crimes, affect our behavior and way of thinking. Because media is very important for our behavior, it can be claimed that the fear of the dark can be strengthened by watching too much horror movies (for instance). All this is not to be dismissed by adults, for it does not concern only children.

All we are human beings, and we have our weaknesses. Everyone fears of the dark, to some degree- some people more, some people less. As Vamshi Krishna remarks: "The creaking of our doors or windows are often ignored during the day but during the night, the same sound drives us crazy. This is because of the anxiety that kicks in due to fear" (Krishna par. 3). The very fact that our senses do not work so well in the dark makes us more unconfident: "Darkness means the inability to see what's happening in our surroundings and that makes us more nervous" (Krishna par. 2). We want to know what is going on out there; we need to have enough information about the environment in which we find ourselves. Still, this fear should not be exaggerated; otherwise one can easily reach the pathological state in which he/she will be afraid of staying alone in the dark (whether in one's own bedroom, or in the street, etc.). As Krishna observes: "Fear of dark as a defense mechanism is okay but if it extends and affects our health causing insomnia we should not overlook it" (Krishna par. 6). We should be careful not to exaggerate our fear of the dark: darkness is a natural condition, although not very pleasant sometimes.

Darkness, as we said, *is associated with the strange, with the mysterious, with the unknown* as well. This is one of the reasons for our interest in the starry sky. The universe is endless, as we are taught; but our mind wants to know all about the universe. Is it really without any limits? Is it endless? What was at the beginning, what will be at its end? What about the stars we see every night? How do they look from close range? We know from our science lessons that stars are too hot and we cannot simply approach them. Still, there is some romantic in watching them and thinking about them: this is due to our curiosity which is made more intensive during the night.

Another positive aspect of the dark is tranquility. Who does not like walking in a warm evening after a hard day at work? Who has not tried to relax, to get rid of all of his/her problems by turning off the lights at home and listening to chill-out music? Sometimes we need to refrain (temporarily) from any thought about our job, about school, about any kind of problems. Darkness provides us with the appropriate conditions. Our brain needs some relaxation as well, and sleep is not the only option to do it. Furthermore, it is recommended to turn off the lights before going to bed; darkness helps us get asleep faster and easier. Light, on the other hand, stimulates our brain and makes our perception more intensive, which in turn prevents us from getting asleep.

These three points related to the psychological dimensions of darkness do not exhaust the discussion among psychologists regarding the dark. In psychoanalysis, light, and darkness symbolize consciousness and the unconscious (or subconscious). Light is mind, intellect, consciousness; darkness is the unconscious, instincts, psychological drives, and so on. Whereas Sigmund Freud himself did not work too much on the psychological dimensions of darkness, his fellow researcher, Carl Gustav Jung, explored this fascinating field. What he found is quite important, and we will turn to it in the next sub-chapter.

2.2 Carl Jung: the Shadow and the Unconscious

Summary:

Carl Jung understands the Shadow as the opposite of the Ego, i.e., of our will, our consciousness. Some claim that the Shadow is our "dark side." Is such an interpretation of Jung's conception correct? As it will be shown, this is wrong- the Shadow also has some positive traits and qualities.

Sigmund Freud and Carl Jung were not the first intellectuals that discovered the existence of the subconscious/unconscious[8]. Long before them, some philosophers asked what the essence of human nature is: whether instincts are our nature; whether there is something beneath the "surface" of our intellect. Thus, it was widely accepted that there is such a part of our psychics, which cannot be explored thoroughly, and which contains our instincts, hidden desires, dreams, forgotten experiences, and so forth. This is the sphere of the subconscious/unconscious.

Carl Jung postulated that our psychics contains models, which he called *archetypes*. These are standard models, which appear in everyone's psychics, without regard to time, place, personal experience. Jung examined their manifestation in dreams, in myths, in folklore traditions, etc. Among them, he listed the archetypes of the Father,

---

[8] Freud used the former term, and Jung- the latter. The difference between both terms is that the subconscious is strictly individual, but the unconscious- collective (common to all human beings).

of Anima, of Animus, and of the Shadow. Archetypes exist independently, which means that we cannot influence their existence. This does not mean, to be sure, that they are of material essence. *They are psychical, but they do not depend on our individual will.* As long as there are human beings in the world, there will be archetypes.

Here we are especially interested in one of these archetypes, the Shadow. In some sense, the Shadow covers all these experiences, emotions, and feelings, which we analyzed in the previous sub-chapter. The Shadow is still not identical with the dark (or with the perception of darkness). It is instead associated with what goes beyond our Ego. For Jung, the Shadow is merely the most significant part of our personality; and the Ego is smaller than it is. How is this possible? Let us see.

Some of Jung's essential ideas regarding the Shadow are exposed in his work *Eion*. He observes there that the Ego is a "complex factor to which all conscious contents are related. It forms, as it were, the centre of the field of consciousness; and, in so far as this comprises the empirical personality, the ego is the subject of all personal acts of consciousness" (Jung 3). *The self is more than the ego.* This difference is significant: we cannot identify the Ego with the self. The Ego is our consciousness, our intellect, our will; it is everything we are aware of. The self, however, includes much more than the Ego. The Ego is our consciousness; its field is very narrow. Still, Jung adds a curious remark regarding the nature of the Ego: "The ego rests on the total field of consciousness, and on the other, on the sum total of unconscious contents" (Jung 4). This means that the Ego has some access to the unconscious. The relations between the two are complicated and are not so easy to conceptualize. What Jung wants to say here is that *the Ego is a necessary part of the self,* and it exists in its relations with what is non-Ego within the self. *There should be a balance between both: consciousness and unconscious, ego and non-ego, reason and emotions*, and so on. Jung is famous for his rejection of the dominating position of the intellect, and the assumption that one can be stable psychically only when there is the proper balance between both parts of one's psyche. He repudiates the idea that humanity's progress can be based entirely on rationalism and intellectualism. On the contrary, he claims, we need to keep our emotions intact, and we have to use our imagination and creativity as well.

What is the self, then? We are used to thinking of it as identical with the ego, at least from other psychoanalysts (such as Freud). *The self is a mystery*; its contents cannot be completely unknown, Jung is convinced. The reason for this is the fact that the self is connected with the collective unconscious, and the latter is endless- it does not end and does not begin anywhere. Consciousness and the collective unconscious, however, should be kept in the proper balance. *The balance between both is called self.*

The self is the most severe problem for contemporary psychology, Jung claims. Whatever we do, whatever we know about ourselves, there will always be something more, something which exists beyond our understanding. Thus, Jung puts limitations to psychology as a science: there is a field which is inaccessible. This field, as other psychologists also assert, is manifested in dreams, in symbols, in our creative activities, and so forth. Their essence is still impossible to grasp. Our self consists of both rationalized contents and symbolic contents. The balance between both is dynamic, it can change over time, but our intellect will never be ultimately victorious in this "struggle." It is important then to admit that ego and self are different things, and the self covers much wider sphere than the ego: "The personality as a total phenomenon does not coincide with the ego, that is, with the conscious personality, but forms an entity that has to be distinguished from the ego" (Jung 5). We have to bear this in mind while discussing the nature of the ego and our consciousness.

What is the relation of this problem with the nature of the Shadow, the reader may ask. The answer is clear: the Shadow is understood by Carl Jung as non-ego, and even as *anti-ego*. It escapes any attempt of the intellect to get to know it in full. This is not all; the Shadow is what we could call our evil side. Given that morality and the ego are interwoven, and our ego bases its decisions on morality, the Shadow is a kind of "rebel" that wants to direct the ego. The direction taken by the Shadow is immoral, and even evil, as we mentioned. As the Swiss psychologist asserts, the Shadow is a "moral problem that challenges the whole ego-personality, for no one can become conscious of the shadow without considerable moral effort. To become conscious of it involves recognizing the dark aspects of the personality as present and real" (Jung 8). There are "dark aspects" of the Shadow, then; but are they absolutely evil?

One of the possible interpretations of these words is the following: we have passions, emotions; we feel hatred sometimes; we want to destroy something, to hurt someone. Maybe this is what Jung has in mind- that the Shadow are all these destructive intentions, thoughts, feelings that we have? This is true to some degree, as we will see. However, the Shadow contains positive contents as well.

Søren Ventegodt and his research team have analyzed the Shadow and its impact on our morality. According to them, *the Shadow is anti-self*, and it is the dark side of every human being. Jung believed they claim, that our moral (good) side should have harmonious relations with our dark side. Unfortunately, because we tend to be moral at every moment and in every situation, these authors remark, there is tension between the ego and the Shadow. This tension increases with every "victory" of morality (or the decisions made by the Ego based on morality); thus the Shadow, in turn, becomes stronger and stronger, and it suddenly "explodes." Then we do things that are otherwise not to be imagined. This is due to our wrong understanding of the self as completely good. Good and evil are relative concepts, and they should be taken as such, according to Jung. The authors add that "a person who chooses to be good is in this phase of his personal growth denying his own hidden evilness, and can now only indirectly observe this denied black side, which appears as evilness and darkness around him" (Ventegodt et al. 1304). As the researcher's team remark, Jung believed "that the shadow, the dark side of man, contains a substantial developing potential that is set free when we attempt to integrate the shadow" (Ventegodt et al. 1303).

In short, the Shadow is not precisely our "evil side." For Jung, *darkness and evil are not the same*. Darkness (in the metaphysical sense) can have its positive attributes. Furthermore, our "dark side" exists independently and autonomously, meaning that it is not completely subjected to our will. We will consider the problem of light in Christian context in the next chapter, but we can already tell the reader that Christianity rejects the reality of evil, therefore the reality of the dark (understood as a metaphor of the evil). Jung himself does not agree with the Christian interpretation of the problem of evil. He turns rather to the philosophy of Gnosticism, a doctrine which was very diverse and had different tendencies and directions. Still, it can be said that Gnosticism in general adhered to ethical dualism, by claiming that good and evil are equally (or almost equally) powerful. However, Jung does not assert that evil is something to be chosen and preferred by human beings; he instead is eager to tell us that evil is relative, and it can be defined only in contrast with our morality. We call evil what does not correspond to our moral norms and values. This still does not mean that there cannot be something good in the values positioned outside of our system of values. Morality is changing, and every person can add new values to his/her moral system of values[9]. Jung refers here to the philosophy of Kierkegaard, who asserted that morality does not encompass everything which is good, and there is some good standing beyond morality (in his case- religion)[10]. Kierkegaard thought that conventional morality is full of hypocrisy, and that all people who are claiming to be moral, are not such; their morality is only formal, it only has an external side. Jung thus does not reject the power of the good. He instead wants to explain that our morality does not include all good in the world, and there can always be something more outside our system of values. The Shadow could help us in the search for new values.

Now, it is essential for us to be aware that we have something more within us, and we need to know more about it. We are not completely good and righteous, and this is in full accordance with every religion in the world, Jung remarks. We should add here that Christianity understands man as having partially sinful nature, so this does not contradict Jung's view regarding the Shadow. The real difference between Jung and Christianity is the fact that for Jung, good and evil are relative, and they interact with each other all the time; the borders between them are not so sharp, and good and evil are sometimes interwoven. By knowing this fact, Jung asserts, we will be able to develop ourselves: "The person who admits that he contains positive as well as negative intentions in his

---

[9] Which does not mean that moral categories are relative. The truth is rather that we need some time to become aware of our worldview and to understand the values we are ready to defend. This takes time and requires a lot of experience.
[10] Since Kierkegaard held that religion stand above morality.

unconsciousness, and strives to embrace both with his existence, can in time observe and acknowledge both sides in himself" (Ventegodt et al. 1304). Instead of adhering to the thought that we are perfect, that we are completely good, we must admit our weaknesses and "dark side."

How can the Shadow be comprehended as having positive attributes, if it is the main force of destruction within us? Ventegodt and his team make the situation even more complicated by asserting that "the center of shadow is the intention destroying the purpose of life most directly, called the anti-life- mission or anti-life- purpose. The shadow therefore appears as a negative copy of the personality" (Ventegodt et al. 1305). What the researchers have in mind is the fact that our life has meaning, and we have to think about it. The Shadow, on the other hand, tends to attack the sense that life has meaning. This stands close to the philosophy of nihilism according to which there is nothing meaningful in the world; the world is either without meaning (Nietzsche) or absurd (Camus). The Shadow puts in doubt all of our values, decisions, and intentions in life.

Notwithstanding, this also plays a positive part: we need to have some doubts about our decisions and our worldview. In such a manner, we can grasp more truths about life and existence. When we are teenagers, we have one worldview; when we are in our 20s, we have another; when we are mature adults, our worldview is much more different than in the beginning. This is due to our life experiences. The Shadow thus helps us understand why life is not what we have expected, and why not all events in our life bring us pleasure and joy. The Shadow, however strange, can assist us in overcoming the life difficulties we have, as the researchers assume: "A lot of people who search for themselves are therefore experiencing great difficulties. At some time, everybody seemingly has to face their dark side- their own shadow" (Ventegodt et al. 1306). Is this true? Are people afraid to meet their own self, to understand more about themselves? This is a fact which cannot be repudiated. Personal growth is a constant process which passes through much suffering. *Suffering and pain make us real personalities.* If our life was full of joy, we would not have been able to understand what is the meaning of life. The presence of suffering, of death, are events that make us think more about life and human existence.

Still, it is not so difficult to stop thinking about the meaning of life. Not few people today try to avoid such questions by giving themselves to fun and pleasures. Actually, this is a victory of the Shadow. We have to balance between our ego and our Shadow, in order to find the meaning of life and to maintain our worldview. As Ventegodt and his team remark: "When the life purpose is clearly admitted and the negative decisions that deny it are found and let go of, the disorder often heals up even when this should not occur according to statistics" (Ventegodt et al. 1310). Our internal dilemmas and hesitations will be eliminated easily in such a manner. This balance is the ideal of many Eastern (Indian, Chinese) religions, as the researchers assert: "The noble art of life called no-mind in the eastern traditions seems to be about suspending reason but to remain good. The famous and rare state of enlightenment seems to follow total integration of the shadow" (Ventegodt et al. 1311). We have to retreat a little from the field of consciousness, of morality, in order to maintain our goodness- such is the absurd conclusion. Still, it can have some value: if we try to suppress our dark side too much, it will "fight" back, and we will lose the struggle.

The integration of our self is significant for Jung, and here he refers to Eastern wisdom. As Ventegodt et al. point out: "It might be that understanding and integrating the shadow, confronting the evil, walking awake into the darkness to win it over, is the straight way to light, joy, love, self-exploration, and in the end healing" (Ventegodt 1311). Our meeting and the acceptance of the Shadow makes it possible for us to overcome the life difficulties, and to realize our reflection on the meaning of life. Not accepting the Shadow, means more tension, more inner conflicts. The way to treat them is to try to find a compromise between our Ego and the Shadow, the Swiss psychologist insists. As the researchers remark: "Only the one who carries the light of consciousness and conquers the darkness of lies and unconsciousness will reach the state of transcendence described by Maslow, or the state of coherence described by Antonovsky, or the state of meaning described by Frankl" (Ventegodt 1311). The key is in the balance of both.

This is only one of the possible interpretations of the archetype of the Shadow. At any rate, Carl Jung himself tried to convince his readers that it is not conceivable to conceptualize the Shadow completely. Hence we cannot define it in full. As Jung puts it: "Although, with insight and good will, the shadow can to some extent be assimilated into the conscious personality, experience shows that there are certain features which offer the most obstinate resistance to moral control" (Jung 9). For example, *projections* are such resistances. If we try to go deeper in our inner self by way of reasoning, we will not achieve anything: the Shadow, and also other archetypes (anima, animus, and others) will resist. This is the nature of the Shadow: it is independent of our will, and it cannot be grasped rationally.

The Shadow is autonomous, and it cannot be simply defined as the lack of the Ego, or deprivation of consciousness. As Jung claims: "Looked at superficially, the shadow is cast by the conscious mind and is as much a privation of light as the physical shadow that follows the body" (Jung 266). Notwithstanding, he goes on, "On closer inspection, however, it proves to be a darkness that hides influential and autonomous factors which can be distinguished in their own right, namely anima and animus" (Jung 266). The Shadow has its own energy, its own capacities, and it can exist without maintaining strong contact with the consciousness. In some sense, it resembles animal instincts: it is "the inferior personality, the lowest levels of which are indistinguishable from the instinctuality of an animal" (Jung 233-4). Still, these definitions are somewhat provisional.

It would be a grave mistake to try to cognize the Shadow: it must be *experienced*, it must be *felt*. On the other hand, if we allow the Shadow to manifest itself more often and more clearly, this will keep the balance between our Ego and the Shadow, ensuing in the integration of the self of which we already wrote: "The more numerous and the more significant the unconscious contents which are assimilated to the ego, the closer the approximation of the ego to the self" (Jung 23). This does not mean, still, that our Ego has to be subordinated to the Shadow. The Ego must, and should be in charge: otherwise, our self will be dissolved, and serious psychic illness will result. As Jung postulates: "It is of the greatest importance that the ego should be anchored in the world of consciousness and that consciousness should be reinforced by a very precise adaptation" (Jung 24). These two parts need to stay in a balanced position. Complete rejection of our Ego, of our consciousness, is wrong, and it should be avoided.

The Shadow is so vital for psychology because it is the closest archetype to the Ego. All other archetypes are more sublime; they are harder to be found and known. For instance, such is the case with anima and animus, two archetypes related to the male and female characteristics of our personalities. As Jung puts it: "Whereas the shadow can be seen through and recognized fairly easily, the anima and animus are much further away from consciousness" (Jung 10). They are also part of our *self*, but still, they are not as important as the Shadow.

The Christian reader may be confused due to Jung's theory of the Shadow as an integral part of the self. We should note here that psychologists do not completely prove the reality of the Shadow. At any rate, it is well-known that we have sinful tendencies and predispositions, so they correspond to what Jung calls the Shadow. Is Christianity wrong because it rejects the positive side of our sinful nature? This is a contradiction: we cannot say that evil is good, and good is evil. Sins must be cleansed, instead of being encouraged. Jung wrongly believed in the truth of Gnosticism and its ethical dualism. Jung saw the Antichrist as the necessary element complementing the Holy Trinity. The eternal struggle between Christ and Antichrist resembles the idea which appears in Zoroastrianism, and which we already discussed. It is not entirely known why Jung took this way- the way of ethical dualism. In all cases, it is clear that he had mystical experiences related to the nature of evil and the necessity of its existence. Still, it is essential to remark once again that *the Shadow is not evil in its essence*; it is rather *destructive*, i.e., *it opposes the Ego*. Both the Ego and the Shadow have positive qualities, although the Shadow can also contain evil intentions and desires. As Jung puts it: "If it has been believed hitherto that the human shadow was the source of all evil, it can now be ascertained on closer investigation that the unconscious man, that is, his shadow…

also displays a number of good qualities" (Jung 266). These qualities include reactions,

instincts, creative impulses, and so forth.

Carl Jung's theory of the Shadow as one of the major archetypes located in the

collective unconscious help us add another dimension to the metaphysical problem of

light: *light as consciousness*, and darkness as the subconscious/unconscious. Besides the

good, light points also to human consciousness. It is often said that the consciousness

sheds light on certain phenomena in the world. On the other hand, phenomena that are

not illuminated by the light of the consciousness, remain "in the dark."

Having analyzed the psychological dimensions of light, we can go further. A

special form of light needs careful elaboration. We already mentioned it, but we have to

carry out an analysis of it. Fire is a form of light, but in some sense it is more than light.

What does "more" mean here? We will turn now to the philosopher Gaston Bachelard to

find the answer.

2.3 Gaston Bachelard: Psychoanalysis of fire

Summary:

Bachelard analyzes fire from a philosophical and poetic standpoint. He describes

various forms and functions of fire, the most important of which are the sexualized fire

and the dynamic nature of fire- fire is related to change, and this makes it so amazing for

us. Fire is not merely a physical substance or process, but it also has psychological and

even metaphysical dimensions.

In a unique work under the title, *The Psychoanalysis of Fire* (1938), the French philosopher Gaston Bachelard exposes the poetic, scientific, and metaphysical dimensions of fire. Fire is a problem, which cannot be examined entirely objectively, because all of us perceive it individually, from our point of view. As Bachelard puts it: "We are going to study a problem that no one has managed to approach objectively…This problem is the psychological problem posed by our convictions about fire" (Bachelard 2). Here the philosopher explains why he has chosen this title for his book: "It seems to me so definitely psychological in nature that I do not hesitate to speak of a psychoanalysis of fire" (Bachelard 2). Still, this does not mean that the psychological explanation is the only one.

On the contrary: fire is universal; it has so many aspects, it is related to so many experiences, feelings, memories, that we cannot narrow it down only to one field. As Bachelard observes: "Fire and heat provide modes of explanation in the most varied domains, because they have been for us the occasion for unforgettable memories, for simple and decisive personal experiences" (Bachelard 7). These domains include art, literature, religion, family life, friendships, science, and so on. The same which we already stated earlier, can be said about fire as well: it is not simply physical substance; it is not merely a subject examined by Chemistry and Physics. Fire has much more connotations, uses, associations. It has spiritual meaning, artistic meaning, religious meaning, and many more.

The first metaphysical meaning found by Bachelard is the *dynamical essence* of fire. Fire symbolizes change. This makes it so unusual for us: the flame is never the same, it is in constant change, in constant movement! The French philosopher observes: "If all that changes slowly may be explained by life, all that changes quickly is explained by fire" (Bachelard 7). Life is also a change, he remarks; but life changes slowly. Life processes pass through gradual modifications. Fire, on the other hand, changes quickly and suddenly: we see the flame now, and just in a while, there are only ashes.

Fire, as Bachelard writes, is different from life: "Fire is the ultra-living element. It is intimate and it is universal. It lives in our heart. It lives in the sky. It rises from the depths of the substance and offers itself with the warmth of love" (Bachelard 7). It is intimate because it is associated with many experiences that are so dear to us. It is universal since it is present universally- not only in the physical (material) world but also in the realm of thought, in the realm of spirit, in the sphere of imagination. It is "ultra-living" because it surpasses life; it is more than life. Non-living matter can also be embraced by fire. If we add heat to the concept of fire, then this idea becomes even clearer: all astronomical objects in the universe are somehow connected with sources of heat (the stars, etc.). Our emotions and feelings related to fire are very often based on our experience of heat and warmth. Fire is development and growth as well, as the philosopher remarks: "Fire is for the man who is contemplating it an example of a sudden change or development and an example of a circumstantial development" (Bachelard 16). This is the dynamic essence and function of fire.

The second point remarked by Bachelard is what he calls "social nature of fire." We usually think that fire is dangerous, and this is its objective quality. Bachelard rejects such a view: "Fire is more a *social reality* than a *natural reality*" (Bachelard 10). At first glance, this sentence is absurd: how can we say that fire is not natural? Bachelard has in mind the fact that children do not know how to protect themselves from fire. They do not know that fire is dangerous. Therefore, this is a fact, which we learn from the others (particularly parents). We learn how to protect ourselves, but we also learn how to kindle the fireplace. At any rate, this is a matter of experience; and other human beings help us understand this experience and conceptualize it properly.

The third point observed by Bachelard is human curiosity, or, what he calls, the Prometheus complex. Prometheus is the Ancient Greek god who, according to the myth, stole the fire from Zeus, and brought it to humanity. Bachelard, however, does not refer precisely to the act of stealing; he defines this complex *as our ability to search for new knowledge*, for new practices; our ability to discover, to invent, to explore. The little child already knows that fire is dangerous. Still, the child is curious and wants to know more about fire. Are there different types of fire? How to light a fire? How to put out a fire? Where does the smoke come from? How many ways to light a fire exist? What is the relation between fire and water (rain)? The child is curious, and in the course of time, it will get more and more information about fire.

Fire here is only a metaphor symbolizing our curiosity, our desire to know, to gain new knowledge, the French philosopher points out. We rely on the knowledge already gained, which our parents and teachers have passed to us: "We propose, then, to place together under the name of the *Prometheus complex* all those tendencies which impel us *to know* as much as our fathers, more than our fathers, as much as our teachers, more than our teachers" (Bachelard 12). The Prometheus complex is essential and inevitable for humanity's progress. It keeps us curious and wondering; it helps us formulate good questions and looking for answers. Prometheus is the symbol of the search for knowledge. This is our, human spirit, the spirit of curiosity.

The fourth point related to fire, according to Bachelard, is the *reverie*. Fire is mysterious, impossible to describe; it is unknown, inexplicable. Fire is another reality for us. No wonder that pyromaniacs exist. As Bachelard claims: "The sight of a fire will cause some man to become a pyromaniac almost as inevitably as a pyromaniac will some day start a fire. Fire smolders in a soul more surely than it does under ashes" (Bachelard 13). Although not all people are pyromaniacs, it cannot be rejected that everyone likes to light a sparkler. By sitting in front of the fireplace at home, we feel physical warmth; and this memory remains forever, especially when we are with our dearest ones. Bachelard here describes his personal experience with fireplaces, and explains that "the fire confined to the fireplace was no doubt for man the first object of reverie, the symbol of repose, the invitation to repose" (Bachelard 14).

The fifth point which we mark here is actually the most important one, in Bachelard's opinion. This is the concept of "sexualized fire." Fire, he claims, has clear *erotic associations*. We often speak of our passions as "fire." *Flames symbolize love*; fire is often related to romantic love. The erotic element cannot be dismissed: passion pass quickly from one stage to another, and its "flames" are put out eventually. To all this, we may add death, however strange: "Love, death and fire are united at the same moment. Through its sacrifice in the heart of the flames, the mayfly gives us a lesson in eternity" (Bachelard 17).

The concept of "sexualized fire" is based on an interesting psychological association. The way in which fire is enkindled, the philosopher observes, resembles a sexual act. Fire is produced- it symbolizes the conception of another human being (a child). Ancient people, he claims, were convinced that there is some analogy between the sexual act and fire. As Bachelard puts it: "If the conquest of fire was originally a sexual 'conquest,' it is not surprising that fire should have remained so strongly sexualized for such a long period of time" (Bachelard 43). Sexual, or erotic associations of fire are also found in paintings and literature, as Bachelard observes, and he gives examples of them. Many symbols are interconnected and interwoven here; the philosopher remarks: "*Sexualized fire* is preeminently the connecting link for all symbols. It unites matter and spirit, vice and virtue. It idealizes materialistic knowledge; it materializes idealistic knowledge" (Bachelard 55). For instance, fire symbolizes the torments, which the wicked will experience in hell; fire is sin, but fire has cleansing power as well. Hence, fire can be understood as the proper way to heaven. Fire is material, but it is also spiritual; it has a sexual character, and still, it has romantic characteristics.

How should we perceive Bachelard's conception of the sexualized fire? His claim that primitive men saw only sexual act in enkindling a fire should be subjected to serious analysis. As a matter of fact, it is hard to believe that primitive men saw precisely this. They were rather amazed by the burning flames and the heat produced by them. In short, fire was a miracle for them. No wonder that they associated fire with divine powers- as it happened in many pagan religions where the main (or one of the major) god symbolized the thunder/lightning. Primitive people had already been acquainted with the presence of natural fire (if we can call it like that) in the world- the sun, the stars, the lightning. They were probably surprised that they were able to light a fire themselves, without the "intervention" of the gods. Hence, the theory that fire was initially seen as sexualized is to be rejected.

Still, Bachelard is right that fire is associated with sin and passions. Human passions really resemble the flames of fire- they burn fast, and then they die down suddenly. Many people do not reflect too much on this fact. They tend to think of passions as long-lasting. This is one of the reasons for having so many disappointments in our life- we rarely discern real feelings (true love, for example) from passions (which are temporary). It is not strange that fire symbolizes both sin and one's cleansing from sins: the sin is consumed in the flames of the passion. In some sense, sin destroys itself. Passion rejects itself; passion is its own opposite, we can say, entirely in the spirit of dialectics.

The purity of fire can be found in one fascinating phenomenon, Bachelard assumes: "The true idealization of fire is arrived at by following the phenomenological dialectic of fire and light" (Bachelard 106). Fire is not identical with flames; there is fire which does not burn, as he asserts: "Like all the dialectics based on perception that we find at the root of the dialectical sublimation, the idealization of fire through light rests on a phenomenal contradiction: sometimes fire shines without burning; then its value is all purity" (Bachelard 106). The shine of such a fire is really incredible: it may burn for a while, but our imperfect senses can not perceive this.

The light shed by the fire is vital for our life. Light not only guides us, help us orientate in the world; it also marks our location, our position, as it was mentioned earlier. Fire is used in emergent situations, for instance when someone is lost in the forest and should give a signal to the rescue team[11]. This can serve as a metaphor for our earthly existence: we need to have fire with us in order to have light. Passion can guide us

---

[11] This example was not given by Bachelard. It is only an interpretation of the sentence above.

through the world. Flames can illuminate the right way, which will take us out of the forest. There are so many paradoxes related to fire, that we cannot list them all, Bachelard says. Fire is a paradox; life is a paradox. Moreover, as the Spanish philosopher Miguel de Unamuno would say, the paradox is life.

This is not all. Fire is more than life, Bachelard says, as we already mentioned. In some sense, fire is life. The French philosopher points out: "The equation of fire and life forms the basis of the system of Paracelsus. For Paracelsus, fire is life, and whatever secretes fire truly bears the seed of life" (Bachelard 73). Fire is dynamics; life is dynamics. Fire is progress, development; life is also progress and development. Fire has a beginning and an end; the same is valid of life. There is still something more to add here: "What I recognize to be living- living in the immediate sense- is what I recognize as being hot. Heat is the proof *par excellence* of substantial richness and permanence: it alone gives an immediate meaning to vital intensity, to intensity of being" (Bachelard 111). We cannot imagine life without heat; we cannot even think of human existence without the availability of heat. *Fire is thus a metaphor of life.*

We will never exhaust all dimensions of fire, Bachelard is convinced. Primitive men perceived fire with reverie. Some researchers explain this reverie with the use of fire, for instance, Frazer (whom we referred to in the previous chapter): "Frazer's whole system of explanation seems to us to be misdirected. Frazer indeed bases his explanations on *utility*. Thus from the bonfires are taken ashes which go to fertilize the fields of flax, wheat and barley" (Bachelard 32). Celebrations involving bonfires are thus to be seen from a psychological standpoint. Every sound explanation should refer to this fact. This is what Frazer dismisses. All experience, feelings, and memories, are essential for human beings. Utility and use of a given object cannot be the basis of its rational analysis. On the contrary, every piece of research needs to understand the way in which human beings perceive fire in different situations, in different contexts. If primitive man had such reverence for fire, Bachelard points out, "it is because he experiences the well-being, the inner and almost invincible strength of the man who is living that decisive moment when the fire is about to shine forth and his desires to be fulfilled" (Bachelard 33).

Here Bachelard comes to an important observation which may shock many philosophers. Various philosophers have proposed Life, existence, reality, the world- all these objects as the first things on which human mind reflected. This is not true, the French philosopher claims, and argues as follows: "We are almost certain that fire is precisely the first object, the *first phenomenon,* on which the human mind *reflected"* (Bachelard 55). Fire is so different from water that this seems logical. Still, one can object to this assertion by turning to the sun and the sky. It is not by accident that the major pagan gods were imagined as living in the skies, and that they symbolized the sun, the thunder, the rain, and so forth.

Contrary to this, Bachelard observes: "That fire is the principle of all seed appears so true to a prescientific mind that the slightest external appearance is enough to prove it" (Bachelard 50). Fire is to be seen as symbolizing the process of production, of causation. This assumption is, still, hard to defend.

Perhaps the last thing which can be said about fire here is its smell. Bachelard himself does not analyze this issue. *However, the truth is that we perceive fire with all of our senses,* and we should not give priority only to its visual form. Let's take for example the smell of a candle in the dark. When the child sees a lit candle, this memory remains forever. The feeling is so strong, because of the light-darkness contrast, and because of the smell. The smell of fire (or candle, or fireplace) is rare because we usually do not live surrounded by fire. The combination of light and the smell of fire (and we can also add the warmth produced by it) is unforgettable. No wonder that candles are so crucial for Christianity- they make us reflect more on the existence. We can see another reality which we usually are not aware of. Candles, particularly in Christianity, are *symbols*- whether of life, whether of our true faith, whether of the connection of God and man. The incense smoke helps us reflect, and it also prepares us for praying. Incense has been important for Christianity from the very beginning, and it is known that this tradition is rooted in an Ancient Jewish tradition. One cannot resist this smell: it is not only strong but also too unusual for us.

If we add the religious images and sculptures to it, the interior of the Christian church, and the melody of the Holy Liturgy, we will find ourselves in another reality, much closer to God. As Emily Sanna observes: "The smoke wreathes around the offering and ascends into heaven. The scent of frankincense starts in the front of the church but eventually permeates to the back row" (Sanna par. 1). Then we start praying, and this is an act which goes smoothly and easily- the incense helps us to do so: "This is prayer of a different sort, prayer that helps us understand faith differently. Our prayers rise up to heaven, like the incense" (Sanna par. 1). The incense smoke makes us realize that the world is not everything which we see, smell, or feel; there is something more, something standing above our daily living. This is our encounter with the Sacred, as Sanna points out: "It reminds a congregation that the entire world is sacred. Both seen and smelled, incense connects our senses to our lives as people of faith" (Sanna par. 5). Candles and incense smoke are an essential part of Christian liturgy- this is a point to which every philosopher dealing with the problem of fire should pay heed.

In conclusion, Bachelard's conception of fire is not homogenous. He instead pays heed to the diversity of its dimensions, to the various ways in which fire can be perceived, felt, remembered, and so on. Fire, he claims, is equally object of science and poetry. *It is wrong to comprehend fire as a mere physical process or object. Fire is more- it exists in our feelings, memories, emotions; it is part of our imagination and creativity.* Fire is present both in our consciousness and in our subconscious. Hence, it is not the job only of scientists to deal with fire, to analyze its cause and the way it is produced. Philosophers, poets, artists, and others, have the same right. Fire is universal, and at the same time, fire is utterly a subjective thing.

2.4 Conclusion

The current chapter has analyzed two main issues: Carl Jung's conception of the Shadow, and Bachelard's theory of fire. As we have seen, light can be associated with our consciousness, to which we can also add our intellect, our mind. Jung believed in the harmony of the opposites. Thus the Ego (our consciousness) and the Shadow can exist together if adequately balanced. Light and darkness, correspondingly, are to be comprehended as interconnected and mutually supporting entities. Furthermore, light, taken in the form of fire, can have additional associations- change, dynamics, life, eroticism, sin, cleansing, and so forth. Unlike light (for example, sunlight), fire can be smelt and touched, which makes it a unique form of light.

One critical dimension of light needs to be analyzed now. We already mentioned the significant part played by candles and the incense smoke in the Christian liturgy. They make us reflect on the essence of this world, and our connection with God. Without a doubt, light is often associated with the divine, with the good, with God. Is there any sound reason behind that? Is light divine, or does it instead points to the realm of the divine? We will try to find the answer in the next chapter.

Chapter III: The Divine light

As we saw in the previous chapter, fire was so amazing for our predecessors, that they believed it has divine power or origin. The sun, in turn, was deified by many pagan religions. Light was understood as having a divine source; if we explore light carefully, we will find the proper way to the divine, people were convinced.

We are already acquainted with Mithraism and Zoroastrianism. Mithra was seen as the sun-god. Zoroastrianism, on the other hand, declared Ahura Mazda as its supreme god, whose essence consists of good, light, wisdom, and so forth. Unlike them, Christianity refuses to identify light with God. Light itself cannot be God; God, of course, radiates light. Now, the problem is as follows: is this light material or not? Does the Divine light exist?

The present chapter will address these two questions. First, we will turn to a fascinating discussion in Byzantine theology, about the reality of the Divine light. The controversy between Gregory Palamas and Barlaam will be presented. Then we will try to elucidate the understanding of divine light in Catholicism. This will help us see light from another- theological- perspective. As it will be shown, the Catholic theology assumes that the true Divine light can be seen only in Heaven, during the state called beatific vision. The chapter will conclude with a short discussion of Mircea Eliade's theory of the sacred and the profane. We will see that light can also be understood as a sacred symbol.

3.1 The Tabor light- a Byzantine discussion

Summary:

This sub-chapter presents an interesting debate on the nature of the Divine light, which took place in the 14th century in Byzantium. Gregory Palamas held that the Divine light is real, and it is part of God's energies. His opponent, Barlaam, claimed that the Tabor light is only a symbol of God's might. The arguments of both sides will be presented.

A theological discussion which has often been dismissed by the researchers of Christianity took place in the 14th century in Byzantium. That was a time when the Ottoman invasion threatened the very existence of Byzantium. In spite of this, theology was still important. The discussion concerned the nature of the Divine light. This is the light which appeared on the Mount Tabor when Jesus was transfigured. Let us turn to the particular passages in the Bible regarding this event:

> After six days Jesus took with him
> Peter, James and John the brother of
> James, and led them up a high
> mountain by themselves.
> There he was transfigured before them.
> His face shone like the sun, and his
> clothes became as white as the light (Matt. 17:1-2).

Moses and Elijah also appeared and began talking with Jesus, in front of the wonderstruck apostles. Peter offers to find shelters for Moses and Elijah. Then God intervenes and speaks to them:

> While he was still speaking, a bright
>
> cloud enveloped them, and a voice from
>
> the cloud said, "This is my Son, whom I
>
> love; with him I am well pleased. Listen
>
> to him!"
>
> When the disciples heard this, they fell
>
> facedown to the ground, terrified.
>
> But Jesus came and touched them.
>
> "Get up," he said. "Don't be afraid" (Matt. 17:5-7).

The description in *Luke* is almost the same, but there is one crucial detail added:

> About eight days after Jesus said this,
>
> he took Peter, John and James with him
>
> and went up onto a mountain to pray.
>
> As he was praying, the appearance of
>
> his face changed, and his clothes
>
> became as bright as a flash of lightning (Luke 9:28-29).

Jesus becomes light Himself; His clothes are very bright. Then Moses and Elijah appear; and then God speaks to the apostles. Jesus, in turn, instructs the apostles not to tell anyone about what they have seen. There are many points to be analyzed here, but what is interesting for us is the light, which appeared in front of the apostles. Was this natural light, or was it divine light?

Two camps opposed each other in this discussion, which took place in the 1340s. On the one hand, there was Barlaam, who claimed that this light was natural and that the description of the Transfiguration was symbolic. His opponent, supported by the monks, was Gregory Palamas. Palamas asserted that the light, with which Jesus shone, was divine light. Barlaam claimed that this is impossible and that in such a manner, Palamas maintains the theory that there is another divinity besides God- the light itself is divine.

The roots of the problem are found in the mystical tradition of *hesychasm*. Hesychasts were Orthodox monks and hermits that devoted their lives to prayer. Some of them claimed that they have seen God radiating Divine light. Now, the task of Palamas was to defend this attitude and to repudiate the accusation of heresy. As John Meyendorf, a renowned scholar in the field of Byzantium writes: "When Palamas defended the 'hesychasts,' his aim was not to defend an imported novelty but to justify what he understood to be well-known and revered tradition, accepted within the mainstream of the Byzantine Church" (Meyendorf 159). This movement was actually not novel, so it did not appear in the 14th century. The term "hesychast" itself described monastic contemplation. Dimitrios Tselengidis, another researcher of Byzantine theology, adds the following: "The main task of the hesychast is the 'guarding of the heart' with the congenial Keeping of the Commandments, spiritual purity, and sacramental life"

(Tselengidis 2). Hesychasts were able to see the Divine light. The hesychast, the researcher observes, "After having surrendered himself to God, sees the glory of God and visualizes the Divine Light. The ultimate purpose of the hesychastic life is for man to become one with the Trihypostatic Monad" (Tselengidis 2). Thus, by contemplating God, one will be able to partake in God's essence, as it was believed then. The Divine light, then, is important to be defined: if it is not divine, then all hopes of the mystics to see God are in vain. Meyendorf remarks that Palamas was accused of heresy due to his conception which sounded "too mystical" at that time.

It should be noted that many heretical doctrines appeared in the Byzantine Empire in the 13th and 14th centuries, and most of them rejected the authority of the Byzantine Church, claiming that one can encounter God only personally, without any need of religious service or ceremonies. The opponents of Palamas held that his ideas stand close to the heretic doctrines popular at that time- the heretics claimed that they had seen God with their eyes (Meyendorf 159).

Another critical detail which can explain the context of the debate is the notion of *theosis* or the assumption that the believer can partake in God, although to some extent. *Theosis* means *deification*. The Orthodox Church was essentially engaged in a discussion regarding the nature of *theosis*. As Meyendorf remarks: "The Greek patristic tradition understands the Christian message as a message of 'deification'… What divinity, then, can be accessible to humans, who are 'deified' in Christ?" (Meyendorf 163). This is a serious issue. If one claims that God is "accessible," then how can we say that God is absolute, that He stands above all Being? Moreover, the other way round- if God is completely "inaccessible," if we can define Him only in negative terms (apophatic theology), then how is this deification achievable? The solution proposed by Palamas, and based on the practice of hesychasm, was the following: there is a difference between God's essence and God's energies.[12] Energies are a manifestation of God; they are the way in which we can approach Him, we can communicate with Him. As Meyendorf explains: "This accessible divine life is defined in Palamism by the terms 'energy' or 'grace'… The divine energy is, indeed, real, 'uncreated divinity'" (Meyendorf 163).

One can still be confused regarding what these energies are. Are they merely manifestations, appearances of God? Is Jesus one of the energies of God? Of course, the answer is negative. Orthodox theology understands the essence of God as His Being. God is what He is. All names, all attributes we ascribe to Him are energies. Gregory Palamas himself points out as follows: "Neither the uncreated goodness, nor the eternal glory, nor the divine life nor things akin to these are simply the superessential essence of God, for God transcends them all as Cause" (Palamas 95). The phrase "superessential essence" can seem absurd, but actually, it focuses on the fact of God's reality, which transcends any Being and any reality (i.e., it is undefinable). Now, the energies are the following: "We say He is life, goodness and so forth, and give Him these names, because of the revelatory energies and powers of the Superessential" (Palamas 95). It is important to note that God's energies, as Palamas thinks, are uncreated; and still, they can have a beginning and an end. This is so because of our own limitations- we cannot grasp God in His very essence. All we can grasp is "around" Him, or His energies. Then, we perceive God as good, but this notion is limited due to our limited understanding of what is good. This is what Palamas means when he writes that "there *are*, however, energies of God

---

[12] Aristotle first used this term. Energy, according to him, is the way in which we practice a given capacity. Thus, it is not the capacity itself (which is seen as passive).

which have a beginning and an end, as all the saints will confirm. Our opponent ... thinks that everything which has a beginning is created; this is why he has stated that only one reality is unoriginate, the essence of God" (Palamas 96). What is "around" God, or the divine energies, are uncreated, and no one would repudiate this fact, he continues. However, God is not only His own essence; He is also the way in which He works- this is *energeia*.

As Meyendorf points out: "God is not limited in his transcendent essence but is also fully and personally existing *ad* extra in his energies" (Meyendorf 164). This *ad extra* allows us to communicate with God, although God stands beyond any Being, including our own existence. This conception makes it possible for theologians, Palamas asserts, to maintain the doctrine of *theosis*, or deification. Meyendorf points out that the real issue was "deification" or man's participation in the Being of God. He remarks: "If that participation is a participation in the *essence* of God, God ceases to be unique in his personal existence" (Meyendorf 164). Such a postulate would distort the true definition of God: if we can enter into His farthest realm, into His real essence, then what kind of essence is this? It will not be of divine character!

The problem of *theosis* does not exist in Catholic theology. What is the reason for that? Catholic theology does not admit any possibility for man to see God on earth. As Meyendorf puts it, Latin theology speaks of beatific vision which is achievable only in Heaven, not in this world; the visions of the mystics are "created grace" (Meyendorf 163). Not that God cannot be seen in any way in this life; but we cannot be certain that we have seen Him in all His might. Due to the differentiation between God's essence and God's energies, the theologians from the Greek tradition were able to explain how people can communicate with God. The Divine light, Palamas postulates, is not natural; it can be seen but not with our senses. *The Divine light is seen with our inner senses.* As Dimitrios Tselengidis explains it: "Being an uncreated glory of God, pre-eternal and infinite, the Divine Light is not sensual, but noetic and spiritual, which is approximated and envisioned spiritually. It is incorporeal divine illumination and Grace" (Tselengidis 3). There is no any doubt, then, that this light is not natural. We do not need our normal senses to see it. We instead need our spiritual senses here. Had this been natural light, everyone would have had the opportunity to see it. However, this did not happen- only the three apostles saw it on the Mount Tabor.

The ethical side of contemplation should be kept in mind. It is vital for one to be a true believer, to give him/herself to asceticism and to make his/her heart pure, as Tselengidis remarks: "Divine illumination to be beheld presupposes the purification of the heart, and it is found evaluatively higher than homiletics about God, and certainly above reason" (Tselengidis 3). Otherwise, one's spiritual sense/s will not develop, and the Divine light will remain unnoticed. This is what hesychasm taught at that time- to be with a pure heart, to try to attain to God by contemplating Him. Tselengidis observes that "the uncreated Grace exists incessantly in the faithful and assists him soteriologically (in matters of salvation) and multifariously, while Her Divine Light illumines him accordingly- at times, more, and at times, less" (Tselengidis 3). By seeing the light, one will become acquainted with the ultimate truth, the truth of our salvation. The sense which is capable of seeing such unnatural light is called *noetic* sense (from the Greek word signifying mental capacity). The light is God's glory at the same time: "This Light becomes visible spiritually with the noetic sense, and it consists of the inseparable glory and brightness of Divine nature" (Tselengidis 3). This completely denies any criticism of the conception that there is light which cannot be seen with our senses. The spiritual sense can also be called noetic, without distorting the meaning of the term.

Not everyone can see the divine light, as it is claimed. The mystics without too much experience will see it only partially. It is essential to have more experience and to practice more the contemplation of the divine light: "In novices for example, the illumination of this Light is dimmer and not constant, whereas in the perfect, in addition to the superabundance of Light, an endowment of humility takes place" (Tselengidis 4). The practice of good deeds requires time, and contemplating the divine light requires plenty of efforts. Purity of the heart is of primary significance. Pride and egoism are obstacles to it, as Tselengidis observes: "Lucifer and our forefathers had the gift of Vision of God. In both circumstances, however, the loss of this charismatic gift took place after their known fall" (Tselengidis 9). Such a gift must be used with wisdom and goodness of the heart: "Lucifer and our forefathers desired and pursued their equality with God, blatantly ignoring their existential specifications as created beings. They proudly and egotistically projected their will; they dodged God and His will for them" (Tselengidis 9). The Divine light was, then, impossible to be seen anymore. This is a gift which we, as humanity, lost, although not for all eternity. Saints and some righteous people can practice this gift, according to the doctrine of hesychasm. Therefore, the doctrine of Gregory Palamas argued in favor of mysticism. This mysticism, to say it once again, was based on the assumption that God is not cognizable in His essence, but can be known partially, in a cataphatic (affirmative) way. As Tselengidis remarks: "While God is unknowledgeable, invisible, and immaterial, He becomes knowledgeable in a supernatural way, contained, translucent, and during *theoptia*, becomes one Spirit with those who accompany Him with a pure heart" (Tselengidis 7).

All these assertions do not sound illogical, the reader can say. What was the reason for Barlaam and his fellows to attack the theory of Gregory Palamas? Did they believe that the divine light exists at all? The argument of Barlaam stands close to the theological movement in the Middle Ages which has been called *nominalism*. In the 13th and 14th century, the Catholic West was focused on the debate between nominalists and realists. Realists claimed that the universals (all abstract entities) exist in reality. Nominalists asserted the opposite- that abstract entities are only names, and that we should search only for particular entities, entities which we can see, touch, speak of, and so on. Both movements existed within the Christendom, and they did not oppose the doctrine of the Catholic Church. Still, they accused each other in distorting the Christian teaching. From the nominalistic standpoint, the Divine light associated with Jesus on the Mount Tabor is simply a *symbol* of the real Divine light, light which is impossible for us to perceive. The apostles thought that they saw the real Divine light, but this was wrong, Barlaam was convinced. The Divine light is merely a symbol likewise, for instance, the lamb of God. God cannot be approached, on the one hand; on the other, our capacities are limited, especially our senses and perceptions. The experience of the mystics only partially reveals the essence of the ultimate reality. Not that their experience is false, or that they lie about it. The truth is that they cannot understand what they have seen themselves, and they need to conceptualize this experience somehow. Moreover, this experience is not susceptible to conceptualization; it cannot be expressed. There are no words which can describe it, Barlaam believed.

Hesychasts did not say anything different. Actually, their point of view regarding the nature of mystical experience completely agreed with such criticism. They still maintained that the Divine light could be seen, and thanks to it, one can approach God, as Tselengidis points out: "The knowledge of God procured by the vision of Light is above all other knowledge, since there is nothing greater in existence than the abidance and manifestation of God inside of us, neither anything equal nor approximate" (Tselengidis 4). Moreover, the very fact that one has seen the Divine light does not mean that one will see it always. This cannot be one's goal in life, as Tselengidis remarks. If we try to devote our life only to see the Divine light, only to partake in God's life, there is a risk to submit ourselves to our own egoistic desires and aspirations. As the Greek researcher writes: "If the faithful pursues *theosis* or the charismatic life of the Spirit and makes it the purpose of his life, he is in danger of succumbing to the same temptation of his forefathers with the analogous consequences" (Tselengidis 9). Deification should be achieved only with God's grace: "*Theosis*, as charismatic life of the Holy Spirit, cannot become man's purpose because man cannot realize a purpose found much beyond and above his created natural capabilities" (Tselengidis 9). We must be humble, we need to be righteous, and to leave God the right to decide what to do with us. Seeing the divine light is not a mechanic exercise; it cannot be simply taught and learned. It is a matter of God's grace, of His own willingness to help us, to guide us, as we will see in the next chapter of this book.

Let us turn now to the arguments used by Palamas himself. He maintains that the Tabor light is (1) described by the Fathers of the Church as Divine light, and (2) has been seen by saints and mystics in their experience. The Tabor light cannot be held to be a separate reality, as some may claim: "If it were an independent reality, eternally associated with Christ in the Age to Come, He would be composed of three natures and three essences: the human, the divine and that of this light" (Palamas 77). Therefore, it is part of the nature of Christ, i.e., of God. Basil the Great,[13] Palamas asserts, writes that this light can be seen with our heart. Palamas explains that "the fact that it is not visible through the medium of air shows us it is not a sensible light. Indeed, when it was shining on Thabor more brilliantly than the sun, the people of the area did not even see it!" (Palamas 80). It is hard to believe that there can be light which is perceivable with our heart, and not with the eyes. However, when we speak about God, there is nothing which can be strange. There is nothing illogical in the assumption that light is not an entirely physical entity, as we have assumed in the present book. The illumination which mystics call light is not very similar to physical light itself; it is rather another type of light which is unknown to ordinary people. This is the noetic senses which we are endowed with. At any rate, it should be clear that the existence of such a sense has not been demonstrated in all human beings. It can be hypothesized, therefore, that only some individuals could develop it. Otherwise, everyone would be able to see the Divine light without serious efforts.

All this does not mean that the Divine light seen by the mystics is always the same. This impression can be produced by the impossibility to describe this experience in full. This light has various forms and appearances, and it cannot be confirmed that the mystics see the same light all the time. As Palamas asserts: "There are numerous

---

[13] He was one of the greatest Greek theologians. His authority was of great importance, and every Byzantine theologian had to refer to him. Basil was the first Byzantine theologian whose works comprised all fields of theology, they included also philosophy and ethics.

differences in the divine vision itself: Among the prophets, some have seen God in a dream, others when awake by means of enigmas and mirrors; but to Moses He appeared 'face-to-face, and not in enigmas'" (Palamas 84). Palamas goes on by referring to the visions of the saints: "Certain saints after the Incarnation have seen this light as a limitless sea, flowing forth in a paradoxical manner from the unique Sun, that is, from the adorable Body of Christ, as in the case of the apostles on the Mountain" (Palamas 88). The symbols of the sea and the sun are, without doubt, only a way to describe these mystical experiences. Light is all that we can grasp from these descriptions. The symbol of the sun resembles many other analogies. Plato in *The Republic* describes a cave with prisoners unable to see real light; and when one of them goes out of the cave, he sees the sunlight and cannot believe it exists. Thus, Plato, as well as other philosophers of the Platonic tradition, understood the ultimate reality as standing beyond our perceptions; only by contemplating we can attain to it. This is the sun of the "true light," as Palamas points out: "For it is another Sun which produces this day, a Sun which shines forth the true light. Moreover, once it has illumined us, it no longer hides itself in the West, but envelops all things with its powerful light" (Palamas 89). This is light coming from the Holy Spirit and facilitated by it. Such a light is not alien to us[14], it is part of our soul: "When, however, the seeing eye does not see as an ordinary eye, but as an eye opened by the power of the Spirit, it does not see God by the means of an alien symbol; and it is then we can speak of sense-perception transcending the senses" (Palamas 90). The latter phrase- "sense-perception transcending the senses"- may sound absurd, but this is the

---

[14] This means, it is not a mere symbol, as Barlaam argues.

way in which mystics usually describe what they have seen. This paradoxical terminology is able better to express their encounters with the divine.

To all this, Barlaam and his fellows replied that even if energies exist, they are created; *ergo*, our contact with them will not help us to enter the process of deification. Barlaam rejected completely the possibility for *theosis* (deification) to take place. We can only imitate *theosis*. Likewise the divine energies imitate (or are analogous to) God's essence. We can partake in God only in Hereafter, not in this, earthly, life. The light of Tabor is nothing but a symbol; it only reminds us of God's power, of the fact that God is almighty. It is entirely wrong to believe that this light represents God's essence.

As we mentioned, the debate was <u>solved</u> on a special Council. The debate itself began in 1337, and the Council started its sessions in 1341. However, the discussion continued for a long time, and it finished as late as in 1351 when the doctrine of Palamas was finally declared being in accordance with the teaching of the Orthodox Church.[15] The Byzantine theory of *theosis* was confirmed, and the practice of hesychasm was officially approved.

Theosis was seen by these theologians as the only way of salvation, as Tselengidis observes: "Those deified are full of the pre-eternal Light which grants them god-like knowledge and life. They are not governed by the created temporal life, having beginning and end, but by the Divine and preeternal life of God the Word residing in them" (Tselengidis 7). It is not easy to know that one has become one with God; but some of the possible signs of this are the following, as Palamas himself writes: "One recognises this light when the soul ceases to give way to the evil pleasures and passions, when it acquires

---

[15] In 1341 the Council decided in favor of Palamas, but this was not the final decision regarding the issue.

inner peace and the stilling of thoughts, spiritual repose and joy, contempt of human glory" (Palamas 90). This assertion reveals the moral basis of the doctrine of hesychasm, which was actually the mighty rival of many heretical teachings. Hesychasm was needed at that time, time of Ottoman conquest and time of intense fight of heretics against the Orthodox Church. It should be noted that the Catholic Church had even more severe problems with heretics in the 14th century, so this was a time of debates and controversies.

The Orthodox teaching of the Divine light has asserted that it was real and uncreated and that it represented the energies of God. On the other hand, the Catholic Church has ignored this debate, because it does not consider the nature of the light of Tabor as a real problem. Its standpoint is close to what Barlaam said- that the Divine light seen in this world is somewhat of a symbolic nature.

In order to advance in our discussion of the theological dimensions of light, we have to turn to some passages in the Bible. We will see there that the concept of the Divine light as understood by Palamas does not correspond to the teaching of Jesus Christ and the apostles. Still, it is hard to reach a final conclusion on the topic.

3.2 Scripture about the Divine light

Summary:

Some biblical passages related to the notion of light will be discussed here. Light is understood in three contexts: as referring to future salvation; as pointing to God's might; and as connected with the beatific vision.

Light is one of the most mentioned words in the Bible. It is used there in various context, some of which include light as a physical substance (as in the Book of *Genesis*), and others- light in a spiritual and metaphorical sense. Three basic ideas regarding the Divine light are found in the Holy Bible:

1. The Divine light as a symbol of the future salvation.

2. The Divine light as a symbol of God's nature.

3. The Divine light as part of the beatific vision.

The idea of salvation and its association with light appears in the Book of *Isaiah*. This is a book generally focused on the hard situation of the Chosen people, and the hope for salvation. The following passage refers to God's Wrath, which will be directed against the Assyrians and everyone violating the Law of God:

> Therefore, the Lord, the Lord Almighty,
>
> will send a wasting disease upon his
>
> sturdy warriors; under his pomp a fire
>
> will be kindled like a blazing flame.
>
> The Light of Israel will become a fire,
>
> their Holy One a flame; in a single day it
>
> will burn and consume his thorns and
>
> his briers (Is. 10:16-17).

Fire is referred to as part of God's punishment of the Assyrians. It should be remarked that earlier in the book, the Assyrians were used by God as His weapon against the wicked ones, including the Chosen people. In this passage, however, God says He will destroy the Assyrians because they are also wicked. God- or "the Light of Israel"- will send fire to destroy the oppressors. This will be a warning to His people, and to all that do not want to listen to Him. God is the hope of the true believers.

The hope of the righteous is the topic of another important passage where the prophet describes the state of salvation:

> No longer will violence be heard in
>
> your land, nor ruin or destruction within
>
> your borders, but you will call your walls
>
> Salvation and your gates Praise.
>
> The sun will no more be your light by
>
> day, nor will the brightness of the moon
>
> shine on you, for the Lord will be your
>
> everlasting light, and your God will be
>
> your glory (Is. 60:18-19).

God will be the *real light* then. This description will appear again the in the depiction of the New Jerusalem in the book of *Revelation*, as we will see later. There is hope for the Chosen people, the prophet says, and the day of joy for the righteous will come. This will be the moment when God and man will be close to each other again when man will have become righteous and will partake in God. The depiction of the New

Jerusalem is not associated with the idea of freedom from any oppressor (Assyrians,

Babylonians, etc.). It indicates instead the freedom of the soul, the joy of being together

with God.

In the *Gospel of John,* we find the second aspect of the theological idea of the

Divine light. John refers to the Divine light as a symbol of God's might at several places.

Christ is the Light of the world; it is emphasized several times there.

> Through him all things were made;
>
> without him nothing was made that has
>
> been made.
>
> In him was life, and that life was the
>
> light of men.
>
> The light shines in the darkness, but
>
> the darkness has not understood it (John 1:3-5).

The words "life" and "light" refer to Christ. Christ is the Light; Christ is our

Savior, this passage indicates. Christ is the truth. Therefore Christ is the Light, and Truth

and Light are identical. Another passage contains the words of Jesus associating light

with life. Here he discusses with some Pharisees, who want to reject His divinity:

> When Jesus spoke again to the people,
>
> he said, "I am the light of the world.

Whoever follows me will never walk in

darkness, but will have the light of life" (John 8:12).

Without a doubt, these words mean that Christ will lead us to Salvation. He does

not mean that He is real light (in the literal sense); this word is employed rather

symbolically. True believers will not "walk in the dark." That is, they will know the

ultimate truth about the world, about the relation God-man, about the Fall, and about

Salvation. *Light and darkness here signify knowledge and ignorance.* The phrase "the

light of life," however, adds another dimension: light is life, light is eternity, and darkness

is death, it is temporality. Believers in Christ will have everlasting life; thus, the Divine

Light will shine upon them.

This is not the only passage speaking of Christ as the Light. The same metaphor is

found in another passage, where Jesus speaks with the crowd:

The crowd spoke up, "We have heard

from the Law that the Christ will remain

forever, so how can you say, 'The Son

of Man must be lifted up'? Who is this

'Son of Man'?"

Then Jesus told them, "You are going

to have the light just a little while longer.

Walk while you have the light, before

darkness overtakes you. The man who

walks in the dark does not know where

he is going" (John 12:34-35).

The light- Jesus Christ- will be with the people for a while. That is, people need to listen to Jesus while they have the chance to do so. Darkness, or ignorance, will follow later, according to His words. The crowd does not believe His words since the crowd believes in the Messiah who will remain on earth forever. The crowd is ignorant and blind; it does not realize that the Messiah has come to earth, that He stands before their eyes.[16]

Can we say that only Jesus Christ is associated with Light in a metaphorical sense? The case is that Christ is the Son of God. Therefore God is Light. However, God as Light is unapproachable; we cannot see Him in this condition. This is confirmed in the following passage from the *First Epistle to Timothy*:

In the sight of God, who gives life to

everything, and of Christ Jesus, who

while testifying before Pontius Pilate

made the good confession, I charge you

to keep this command without spot or

blame until the appearing of our Lord

Jesus Christ,

which God will bring about in his own

---

[16] One of the fundamental points of disagreement between Christianity and Judaism is the fact that the latter does not recognize Christ as the Messiah.

time- God, the blessed and only Ruler,

the King of kings and Lord of lords,

who alone is immortal and who lives in

unapproachable light, whom no one has

seen or can see (Tim. 6:13-16).

This passage evidently indicates that God's Light cannot be seen; at the same time, it is written that He will send His son (the Second coming of Christ). Why not interpret this text as meaning that Christ is the approachable Light? Because of His double nature- (fully) divine and (fully) human- Christ can also shine with light which can be seen by human beings. Thus, there is some room for the theory of Palamas that the Divine light can be present during some mystical experiences. Still, the passages quoted here do not confirm that.

The third use of the notion of light in the Bible is the Last Judgment and humanity's existence after it. This is described in the last two chapters of the Book of *Revelation*, where the heavenly Jerusalem is depicted. The righteous will inhabit the heavenly Jerusalem, which is an allegory of Heaven. The existence there is compared with light shining bright:

The city does not need the sun or the

moon to shine on it, for the glory of God

gives it light, and the Lamb is its lamp.

The nations will walk by its light, and

> the kings of the earth will bring their
>
> splendor into it.
> On no day will its gates ever be shut,
>
> for there will be no night there.
> The glory and honor of the nations will
>
> be brought into it (Rev. 21:23-26).

The natural sunlight will not be needed; this is another reality where people will have another source of light. The Lamb of God is the lamp, i.e., it is the instrument of God which radiates light everywhere. Light can be understood in both senses here: in a metaphorical sense (as pointing to the righteousness of the souls inhabiting Heaven), and in a transcendent sense (as describing a state of affairs which our mind cannot comprehend). The latter stands close to the interpretation of Gregory Palamas. This is the beatific vision: *a state in which the soul experiences amazing joy*. It is compared to an everlasting day. As it is written, there will not be night anymore:

> No longer will there be any curse. The
>
> throne of God and of the Lamb will be in
>
> the city, and his servants will serve him.
> They will see his face, and his name
>
> will be on their foreheads.
> There will be no more night. They will
>
> not need the light of a lamp or the light

of the sun, for the Lord God will give

them light. And they will reign for ever

and ever (Rev. 22:3-5).

Here light is goodness, righteousness, justice, joy. Darkness will disappear completely. There will not be any evil, any suffering, any sin anymore. This the optimistic vision presented in the book of *Revelation*. The book itself depicts a vast transformation of our present world into the world ruled entirely by God and the righteous ones. It resembles the vision of prophet Isaiah, who described the coming of the new world, a world ruled by justice and wisdom and deprived of any sin. In the book of *Revelation*, light is not merely a symbol; it is depicted as real, true Light radiated from God. However, it can be said that the New Jerusalem actually depicts the state of beatific vision.

The passages quoted in the present sub-chapter do not show clearly whether the light, which the apostles saw on the Mount if Tabor, was perceived with their senses, or it was entirely spiritual. The Orthodox theology assumes without a doubt that the apostles perceived the light with their inner senses, but the light itself was not entirely spiritual, so it also had physical dimensions. The Tabor light was another type of light, light which we do not see very often (and many of us will never see in this earthly life). The passages demonstrate clearly that this phenomenon was unique due to its connection with Jesus Christ, and that Jesus shone with this light intentionally, by His own will.

Now, in order to understand better the nature of this light, we will turn to the Catholic conception of the Transfiguration. What do Catholic theologians think about the Transfiguration?

3.3 The Catholic understanding of the Divine light

Summary:

The problem of the Tabor light has not been examined comprehensively by the Catholic theologians. The Catholic conception of the Divine light postulates that it can be seen only in Heaven, in the state called beatific vision. The present sub-chapter discusses in short what is the nature of this beatific vision. Additionally, it explains what Christ's Transfiguration and why it is important for Christianity is.

Orthodox theology is based on mystical practices, or at least it is prone to mystical tendencies. Unlike it, the Western rationalization prefers interpreting the act of Transfiguration rather as a symbol. Symbol of what? Is it a symbol of God? Is it a symbol of Christ's role for the salvation of humanity? Transfiguration, according to the interpretation of Catholic theologians, symbolizes the future salvation of humanity. It reveals to the apostles the fate of Christ and the suffering to which He will be subjected. *The Transfiguration also shows that Christ is of divine nature.* This was the first case when His apostles began realizing that He is the Son of God. Hence, the light of the Mount of Tabor refers to the future salvation. It also refers to the beatific vision, which will be discussed later in the present sub-chapter.

The term *transfiguration* comes from the Latin word meaning "to change the shape of something." In some sense, it is similar to the word transformation, but with one important difference: the latter term indicates that a certain person changed entirely and forever. It also indicates that the physical appearance of the person changed. On the other hand, the term *transfiguration* was seen as the proper term, which can describe the phenomenon seen by the apostles. The Transfiguration of Christ was thus temporary; it was an act which revealed the divine essence of Christ for a while. This act is described by the Catechism of the Catholic Church as follows: "For a moment Jesus discloses his divine glory, confirming Peter's confession. He also reveals that he will have to go by the way of the cross at Jerusalem in order to 'enter into his glory'" (Catechism 555). The Glory of Christ is the inner, divine light which can be seen only with man's inner senses. This is a situation which, the Catechism claims, is important not only because of the amazing light radiating from Christ. It is of primary significance because then He declared that His suffering will begin soon and that they must be prepared for it. As it is summarized in the Catechism: "The Transfiguration gives us a foretaste of Christ's glorious coming, when he 'will change our lowly body to be like his glorious body'" (Catechism 556; the latter phrase refers to Phil. 3:21).

Steven Williams emphasizes the importance of the Transfiguration. According to him, this event is so special that it does not deserve to remain dismissed by the Western theologians. The synoptic gospels, he asserts, contain only two episodes when the Voice of God is heard: "The first time is at the baptism, the second at the transfiguration of Jesus Christ. If the baptism signifies and initiates the opening phase of Jesus' public ministry, the transfiguration apparently inaugurates the next, climactic phase" (Williams

14). The climactic phase is the suffering of Christ, His death, and His Resurrection. It is completely wrong to claim, Williams says, that the authors of the gospels confused these two events- the Transfiguration and the Resurrection. As he points out, "over the years a number of scholars have supposed that the transfiguration story common to the synoptics is a misplaced resurrection account" (Williams 15). This theory assumes that "originally it circulated as a story of a resurrection appearance, but at some stage it became attached to the earthly ministry of Jesus and was transfigured into the form in which we now encounter it" (Williams 15). We do not have arguments in favor of such a hypothesis. If we reject the historical reality of the Transfiguration, then we should reject the reality also of the death of Christ and His Resurrection, Williams remarks. It is a historical event, and without a doubt it can be interpreted in several ways; but it really occurred and was described by Mark, Matthew, and Luke.

Regarding the meaning of the Transfiguration, Williams expresses his agreement with the traditional understanding of it: "The transfiguration is a sign, anticipation, installment or foretaste of the glorious manifestation of the Son" (Williams 22). Here we see that the Transfiguration is interpreted as a sign pointing to the future salvation. The problem of the essence of the Tabor light is not considered in depth. Still, Williams remarks, recently there has been some interest in this event. Various interpretations have appeared, but none of them refers to the Transfiguration as the moment when real divine light shone and was seen by the apostles.

There are two central approaches to interpret the Transfiguration of Christ: subjective and objective. The subjective approach analyzes only what the apostles saw and heard. The objective approach, on the other hand, has to explain the event in its historical dimensions: when it happened, where it took place, and so forth. The first approach is more popular, because of the lack of sufficient objective information in the New Testament regarding this event. From a subjective point of view, Williams observes, "The disciples were given a vision by God which allowed them to see something of the significance and glory of Jesus. This could have been given to three of them on the mountain top, as recorded. But vision it was" (Williams 17). The important thing here, he claims, is the part played by God: He intervened by speaking to the apostles. This shows the direct connection between God the father and Christ.

Furthermore, we cannot say anything about the physical transformation of Christ; we only know what the apostles saw themselves: "It was not an objective transformation of Jesus' physical countenance and material body" (Williams 17), as the researcher points out. From such a standpoint, we cannot say what the nature of the light was. Therefore, the Palamas' theory of the Divine light cannot be confirmed by referring to the Bible itself.

God here reveals that Christ is His Son, the researcher remarks. The Ancient prophets appear here as to make legitimate the words of Christ that He is the Savior (Messiah). The light radiating from Christ is the light of His Divinity. In such a manner, Christ demonstrates His being the Messiah in a twofold way: first, by referring to the Ancient prophets and the Ancient Israelite tradition; and second, by a miracle which remains inexplicable to the apostles. As Williams puts it: "The transfiguration account, by not just setting him in the company of Moses, but by exalting him more highly, is supremely the revelation of the divine sonship of Jesus, which is what the voice from heaven proclaimed" (Williams 24).

Regarding the first point, Williams writes: "Jesus' ministry invited the question of his relationship to Moses and the law" (Williams 24). This exceptional event had to open the eyes of the apostles. Still, it is interesting why Jesus told them to keep the event in secret? There can be plenty of explanations. One of these is the fact that by knowing He is the Son of God, some people could try to prevent Him from accomplishing His mission. It was too early even for the apostles to know the truth, so Christ asked them to be silent.

The Western Christianity, Williams remarks, does not pay too much heed to the mystical side of this event. Its symbolism is what has interested the theologians. No doubt, some of the experiences of the mystics may resemble this one; and still, the Transfiguration is important because it is the message of Christ that He is the Savior, and that He has come to us, that He is among us. As Williams points out: "In relation to Christian mysticism, what is significant about the transfiguration is not what it might have in common with mystical experiences, but its specific revelation of Jesus Christ" (Williams 16). He adds further: "'This is my Son, whom I love' or 'my Son, whom I have chosen' says the voice from heaven, in a way that distinguishes Jesus from the greatest of mystics in the Christian tradition" (Williams 16).

The other important point needing examination is the problem, whether the Divine light can be seen on earth. Catholic theologians do not exclude this option. Still, as we proved, the Tabor light remains a symbol for Christians: a symbol of Christ's Passion and Resurrection; a symbol of the destiny of man- to take the way of Christ; and symbol of the forthcoming Judgment Day. It even can be assumed that the Transfiguration marks the turning point in man's history: from that moment on, humanity has started turning to God by realizing the divine presence in this world. We know that God is here, with us, and He is observing us; we know that the Judgment Day will come and that no one will escape from it.

What about man's existence in Hereafter, then? Without a doubt, the majority of theologians agree that the Divine light can be seen and enjoyed there by the righteous souls. This process will start first with the resurrection of the righteous (who will have new, glorious bodies), and then with their judgment. Being sent to Heaven, they will enjoy God's presence, God's love, and God's wisdom for all eternity. Heaven is associated with the sun, with light, with the angels shining bright, with God sitting on His shining throne, etc. It is good to remind the reader that the Christian understanding of Heaven does not see it as a physical place (i.e., having physical dimensions); *it is instead a spiritual state*. It is wrong to think of Heaven as located somewhere above us, up in the skies. Hence, the light described in the Bible and the theologians is not of physical nature. It is the light depicted by the hesychasts and other Christian mystics. This light is spiritual; it is not perceived with our ordinary senses. From such a standpoint, there is no logic in the atheists' argument that Christianity describes Heaven naively. Rather, atheists are naïve, for they think of Heaven in material terms. Heaven, as it is written in the Catechism of the Catholic Church, is "this perfect life with the Most Holy Trinity - this communion of life and love with the Trinity, with the Virgin Mary, the angels and all the blessed" (Catechism 1024). What is important in this definition is the co-being of the righteous with God and the angels. It is a state of affairs, and not a place. It is associated, however, with positive feelings and emotions: "Heaven is the ultimate end and fulfillment of the deepest human longings, the state of supreme, definitive happiness"

(Catechism 1024). They are only provisional, still: we cannot describe the real joy of the righteous in Heaven. We can only speak in approximate terms, terms which are analogous to the state of existence of the righteous in Hereafter. As it is written: "This mystery of blessed communion with God and all who are in Christ is beyond all understanding and description. Scripture speaks of it in images: life, light, peace, wedding feast, wine of the kingdom, the Father's house, the heavenly Jerusalem" (Catechism 1027). The description of the Heavenly Jerusalem was already referred to in the present chapter, but we can add that it is not a place; it does not have anything common with the real (earthly) Jerusalem. It is rather an analogy which aims at clarifying the essence of the new state of affairs which will appear after the Judgment Day. The new man will be "born," the man who will return to his real home, to his co-being with God. New Heaven and New Earth will appear, which means that the whole world will be transformed. This, of course, does not indicate that the material world will disappear completely since the bodies of the righteous will be resurrected. However, the latter will continue their existence in a new form, as glorious (resurrected, incorruptible) bodies.

Another dimension to be added to the Christian conception of Heaven is the fact that it is constituted by God, the angels, the blessed ones, and the righteous. As it is said in the Catechism: "The life of the blessed consists in the full and perfect possession of the fruits of the redemption accomplished by Christ… Heaven is the blessed community of all who are perfectly incorporated into Christ" (Catechism 1026). Heaven is the state in which, as we mentioned, the righteous partake in the eternal life[17] of God. Therefore, there is unity of man and God: a unity which restores the initial condition of existence of

____

[17] The phrase "eternal life" is nothing but a metaphor here, for God's reality goes beyond any form of Being, of existence, of living.

man as standing close to the divinity. Let's recall that the creation of the world started with God's words "Let's there be light!" (Gen. 1:3). Light is thus understood as the initial condition of existence of the world. There is nothing strange, then, that restoring the same (spiritual) light is one of the occurrences during the state called Heaven.

The French theologian Reginald Garrigou-Lagrange added interesting remarks regarding the nature of the glorious light in Heaven. Defining what is the beatitude which the righteous will experience in Heaven, he observes: "Celestial beatitude is the consummation of that transforming union, spoken of by St. Theresa and St. John of the Cross the consummation of that vision wherein the just soul is deified in its very depths" (Garrigou-Lagrange 5.28[18]). The beatific vision cannot be compared with any earthly experience- it is wrong to identify it with the experiences of the mystics. Here is why: "It surpasses by far all vision, even the intellectual visions which the great mystics receive here on earth, because these visions remain within the order of faith and do not give intrinsic evidence of the Trinity" (Garrigou-Lagrange 5.29). In brief, the beatific vision is true in its essence; and mystical experiences are vague, they do not allow us to know a lot about God. These experiences are like a candle in the night: they radiate some light, and it is enough to guide us. However, the candle itself cannot illuminate everything around us. Therefore, all descriptions offered by Christian mystics should be understood only as analogies or allegories of the essence of beatific vision.

Another difference is the fact that on earth we can have some knowledge of God only by referring to His creation: by observing nature; or by reflecting on our own nature. In such a manner, our knowledge of Him is distorted. The beatific vision lacks this

---

[18] The first number refers to the particular part of the book, and the second number- to the number of the section.

defect, as the French theologian asserts: "We are called to see God, not only in the mirror of creatures, however perfect, not only by His highest radiations in the world of angels. We are called to see Him without the medium of any creature" (Garrigou-Lagrange 5.29). This is an immediate vision which does not require the help of other beings or other kinds of mediums. It is absolutely true in its nature, but still, we cannot know God absolutely- for our abilities will still be inferior to His powers. We will see not only the energies of God- as Palamas would say- but His essence as well. The energies can lead us to Him, but this will never suffice to know God, to have appropriate knowledge of Him. God has to help us to get even some knowledge. The beatific vision is not our own effort; it is the outcome of God's love and grace for us. This grace takes the form of the glorious light, as Lagrange claims: "Any created intelligence therefore needs a supernatural light to elevate it, to fortify it, that it may be able to see God as He is in Himself. Otherwise it would be before Him as the owl before the sun" (Garrigou-Lagrange 5.29). This proves that we cannot do it ourselves; this is beyond our powers.

Light is, therefore, necessary to gain this knowledge. Not only the intellect is enough; we need the Light of Glory (or the Divine light, as Gregory Palamas calls it): "The beatific vision arises from the intellectual faculty as its radical principle, and secondly from the light of glory as its proximate principle" (Garrigou-Lagrange 5.29). How does this works? Why is this light needed at all? Garrigou-Lagrange explains it in the following way: "This light supernaturalizes the vitality of our intelligence, as the infused virtue of charity supernaturalizes the vitality of our will" (Garrigou-Lagrange 5.29). Whether we will have access to God's glory, thus, is His decision: we cannot do it alone, only by ourselves. This is important, and it should be kept in mind. For instance, the representatives of the movement called The New Age, assert that one can attain to God himself, with many efforts; but this is a process which does not depend on the will of God! There are certain practices and "exercises," they say, which can help us obtain the necessary knowledge about God, and we can thus even partake in Him through these practices.

It should be noted that in such case, the practitioner will only encounter himself (maybe- his inner Self), but he will not encounter the real and true God. The Light of Glory comes from without, and not from within; it is not located in our inner Self. Of course, our will and efforts are needed, but they are not enough. God's grace plays the decisive part here, as Garrigou-Lagrange claims: "The light of glory and infused charity, thus received into our two higher faculties, themselves arise from the consummation of sanctifying grace" (Garrigou-Lagrange 5.29). From such a standpoint, hesychasm and all other Christian mystical teachings should not be considered as "techniques" for attaining to God- such "techniques" are only illusion and self-deception. There are some methods, of course, for experiencing the energies of God, as the Orthodox theologians assert; still, these methods do not work perfectly and do not guarantee that one will really experience the Divine light, the divine power.

The beatific vision is the only state in which a human being can encounter God and know Him, although not entirely and absolutely (for, only God knows Himself absolutely). The Divine light is manifested in its entirety only in this condition, according to Catholic theology. Still, some earthly manifestations of it are possible, as we will see in the concluding chapter of this book.

Before turning to the problem of the mystic experience and the presence of Divine light, it will be good to add another dimension to our examination of the metaphysical aspects of light. Light, and all phenomena connected with it can be seen as a sign pointing to the Sacred.

3.4 The Light as the Sacred

Summary:

Here the theory of Mircea Eliade of the sacred and the profane will be employed as the basis for understanding light as sacred and as a symbol of the sacred. We have forgotten the old worldview of the world as sacred, Eliade claims, and it is essential to understand what our predecessors (*homo religiosus*) thought about the world.

By now we have written about the Divine. Still, there is another concept which needs to be clarified- the concept of the sacred. The difference between both is that *the sacred is not the divine itself. Sacred can be an entity, a thing, a process, which point to the divine*; but they are not identical with the divine itself.

In the first chapter of the present book, we analyzed some religious conceptions of light. It should be clear that the practices described there are devoted to the sacred. Still, we did not discuss there these practices but as connected with the cult of light, the cult of the sun. In the present sub-chapter, we will build upon the theory of Mircea Eliade, one of the most prominent researchers of religion. Eliade analyzes the problem of the sacred, and especially how the religious mind sees the world. According to Eliade, there are two modes of being: sacred and profane. Eliade aims at proving that the emergence of the profane is a recent phenomenon.

The profane is typical of the modernity, and especially of the 19th and 20th centuries. In his book *The Sacred and the Profane*, Eliade asserts that "The completely profane world, the wholly desacralized cosmos, is a recent discovery in the history of the human spirit" (Eliade 13). Prior to this, the world was seen as sacralized, as having sacred character. What does this term mean? According to the definition given by Eliade: "*Homo religiosus* always believes that there is an absolute reality, the sacred, which transcends this world but manifests itself in this world, thereby sanctifying it and making it real" (Eliade 202). The world is sacred, which means, the world is full of signs pointing to the gods (to the divine)[19]. There are many places related to the deeds and actions of the gods, the religious man believes. Every single occurrence, every phenomenon is a sign of the will of the gods. The world contains many signs, and all we need to do is to read them properly. The profane man, or rather the modern man, who adheres to the principle of profanity, rejects such a worldview: "Modem nonreligious man assumes a new existential situation; he regards himself solely as the subject and agent of history, and he refuses all appeal to transcendence" (Eliade 203). There is nothing beyond what we can see, experience, perceive, etc. The world is completely natural, it does not contain any supernatural forces, any god, any divinity. All beliefs and convictions of the religious people are to be considered superstitions, which are not founded in the objective world.

---

[19] Eliade speaks in general about the religious mind. This is the reason for his generalization by using the phrase "the gods." Polytheism has much longer history than monotheism, according to him and other researchers of religion.

This is the mentality of the modern, profane man. All objects, considered sacred, are thus taken as having no value.

This approach to the essence of the world is wrong, Eliade remarks. Even though many people (especially in the United States and in Western Europe) are prone to atheism, they still are subjected to beliefs they are not aware of. One of the examples is Marxism;[20] there are also other ideologies, which can be given as examples of such religious attitude, which is not realized by the modern man. Many scientific theories are not strictly evidential, thus they are based on pure belief. For instance, both the theory of evolution and the theory of the Big Bang are products of hypothetical assumptions, since human beings can not witness them. Our religious mentality should be implemented in some way. As Eliade puts it: "Profane man is the descendant of *homo religiosus,* and he cannot wipe out his own history- that is, the behavior of his religious ancestors which has made him what he is today" (Eliade 209). The conviction that today's man is completely rational is an empty and futile view: "A purely rational man is an abstraction; he is never found in real life" (Eliade 209).

There was a time when the religious ideas were transformed into philosophical ones, Eliade writes. Without any doubt, with the emergence of abstract thinking and systems of abstract concepts, the sacred was gradually modified. This was the beginning of the process of *profanization*, or *desacralization*. The desacralization of the sun as a divinity began in the 5th-6th centuries AD, as Eliade remarks: "In the Emperor Julian's treatise *On the Sun King*, as in Proclus' *Hymn to the Sun*, solar hierophanies give place to *ideas,* and religious feeling almost completely disappears after this long process of

---

[20] Marxism, Eliade observes, is based on the Messianist view typical of Judaism and Christianity. It believes in the future "salvation" (the victory of the *proletariat*).

rationalization" (Eliade 158). This is only an example of the transformation of religious ideas into philosophical (abstract) ones.

Hierophany is a term employed by Eliade to signify the manifestation of the sacred. According to the definition given by him: "To designate the *act of manifestation* of the sacred, we have proposed the term *hierophany*. It is a fitting term, because it does not imply further; it expresses no more than is implicit in its etymological content, i.e., that something sacred shows itself to us" (Eliade 11). This term should replace the term *theophany* or manifestation of God/the gods. The sacred appears, and this is a fact. However, we have to ask now: why and how does the sacred appear? The religious (or mythological) mind believes that there is a permanent presence of God/the gods on earth and in the whole universe.[21] These gods communicate with human beings; they leave some material objects on earth. These objects, in turn, become sacred because the gods possessed them. In such a way, one can explain why Zoroastrianism has a cult of fire; why fire must be present in every Zoroastrian temple. All objects resembling sun or sunlight could be used as signs pointing to the sun-god, in a similar fashion. Such an object is sacred because it is associated with divine powers; and the opposite of it is called *profane*. Hence, not the whole world was sacred for our predecessors, Eliade maintains. There were only a few sacred objects.[22] However, people believed that they are really connected with the divinity. As the French and Romanian researcher claims: "Man becomes aware of the sacred because it itself, shows itself, as something wholly different from the profane" (Eliade 11). Normal objects thus are transformed into special

---

[21] We have to keep in mind that the concept of the endless universe is comparatively new, it has been formulated since the 1950s and 1960s.

[22] The more sacred objects exist in the world, the bigger will be their insignificance. Sacred objects are valuable because they are rare.

ones, into sacred objects: "The sacred tree, the sacred stone are not adored as stone or tree; they are worshipped precisely because they are *hierophanies*, because they show some thing that is no longer stone or tree but the sacred, the *ganz andere*" (Eliade 12).

The transcendence thus becomes imminent; the ultimate reality becomes part of our own reality, the reality we experience and we live in. What is remarkable here is the fact that every material object could become sacred, and there is no exception to this rule. Evidently, there are objects, which are used more often as sacred- fire (or bonfire), trees, hilltops or mountain tops, religious images, and others. They have special symbolic content- for example, hilltops and mountaintops are the "connection" between earth and heaven, thus allowing for the easy "communication" between man and the gods. Both realities "contact" each other, and the ultimate reality "goes down" to earth. As Eliade asserts: "In each case we are confronted by the same mysterious act- the manifestation of something of a wholly different order, a reality that does not belong to our world, in objects that are an integral part of our natural 'profane' world" (Eliade 11). *The function of the sacred is to orientate man in the world, and to show him how to manage with various real life situations*, Eliade maintains. Thanks to the sacred, the world has meaning and order: "The sacred reveals absolute reality and at the same time makes orientation possible; hence it founds the world in the sense that it fixes the limits and establishes the order of the world" (Eliade 30).

Some of the most important sacred objects were the astronomical ones, especially those located near the planet Earth. Not only the Sun but also the Moon provoked the interest of ancient people. There were plenty of cults related to the Moon. Eliade maintains that due to these cults, man was able to connect various life events with each other: "It was lunar symbolism that enabled man to relate and connect such heterogeneous things as: birth, becoming, death, and resurrection… the cosmic darkness, prenatal existence, and life after death, followed by a rebirth of lunar type" (Eliade 156). The very idea of cycle appeared due to the observations of the Moon phases. It can also be claimed that the first calendars were based on these phases. In short, the lunar symbolism was related to the conviction that life changes, and at the same time that everything disappears and appears again and again, and this cycle never ends.

Interestingly, Eliade points out, "The moon confers a religious valorization on cosmic becoming and reconciles man to death" (Eliade 157). On the other hand, the sun is seen as a symbol of eternity. It is always the same; it always shines brightly during the day; we know that it will appear again tomorrow. As Eliade puts it: "The sun does not share in becoming; although always in motion, the sun remains unchangeable; its form is always the same. Solar hierophanies give expression to the religious values of autonomy and power, of sovereignty, of intelligence" (Eliade 157). The sun, then, is seen as constant and immutable. The Moon is rather associated with mystery, with changes, with something strange and unknown.

Now, let us try to build on Eliade's theory of the sacred and the profane. Light is seen in the profane sense nowadays. It is considered to be a purely physical thing. Only physicists can deal with it; it is their task to examine it, it is said. If we perceive light as having a metaphysical basis, as existing not only in this world but also as having another reality, then we will see it as something metaphysical. This does not lead automatically to the understanding that light is sacred. One more thing is missing. What is it? In order to be sacred, a given object must be associated with God/the gods/the divine. Light, then, should be either connected with God or should be taken as part of God (from a Christian standpoint). The discussion of the Tabor light demonstrates that light is somehow part of God (of God's energies). Hence it is sacred. However, not every light is sacred. This is only the light on Mount Tabor, for instance. The religious mind could not accept the view that all objects of the same type are sacred at once. Not all trees are sacred, but only a few; not all mountains are sacred, but only few of them; and so forth. Therefore, it is essential to make things more precise by stating that light can point to God, but not every type of light is related to God. The fact that we enjoy sunshine does not mean that we get closer to God. This light should have a special nature — such light we can encounter, for example, in a beautiful Gothic church; or in a candle; or a religious image (icon). In the following chapter, we will see that there is special light, which can lead us to God- this is the light experienced by the Christian mystics.

One question, which could be asked, is the following: is the sacred object real? Is there any sacred reality? Can we demonstrate that such a reality is objective, that it is independent of any mind and perception? As a researcher of religion, Eliade is not able to provide us with a precise and reliable answer. The task of the researcher is to examine the roots of the process. Whether the sacred reality is real, is not a task of any researcher. What Eliade offers his reader, is the fact that such perception of the world exists and that it makes some difference in the life of the individual. As he puts it: "The existence of *homo religiosus* especially of the primitive, is open to the world; in living, religious man is never alone, part of the world lives in him" (Eliade 166). The presence of the sacred makes our life meaningful. We are aware of the fact that we are not alone, abandoned in the world (as some atheists have claimed). We are confident that there is divine power, which takes cares of us and will never abandon us.

Let us turn to our feelings related to the encounter with the sacred. The sacred provokes various feelings in us. The first we feel is awe. We realize that our being in this world is limited, that we are finite beings. The sacred, on the other hand, is endless; it does not have definite borders. An excellent example of this kind of awe is the scene with Moses and the burning bush. Moses decides to see what is going on, and then he hears the voice of the Lord:

> So Moses thought, "I will go over and
> see this strange sight-why the bush
> does not burn up."
> When the Lord saw that he had gone
> over to look, God called to him from
> within the bush, "Moses! Moses!" And
> Moses said, "Here I am."
> "Do not come any closer," God said.
> "Take off your sandals, for the place
> where you are standing is holy ground."
> Then he said, "I am the God of your
> father, the God of Abraham, the God of
> Isaac and the God of Jacob." At this,
> Moses hid his face, because he was

afraid to look at God (Exod. 3:3-6).

No one can see the face of God. This means, no one could ever know the essence of God. This encounter of Moses with God is an example of one's experience with the sacred. This is the reason for Moses hiding his face from God. The power of the divine is strong. The same can be said about the power of the sacred places. The only difference is that believers do not need to hide their faces. They can feel the presence of the divine without being shocked or afraid.

The sacred can provoke pleasant feelings as well. We can feel joy and relaxation while visiting a sacred site. Entering a church, we can feel a special atmosphere there. The religious images, the light of the candles, the smell of incense- all of them affect our feelings and mental state. This atmosphere helps us reflect better on the meaning of life, on our relation with the divine, on our life mission.

Mircea Eliade's theory of the sacred improves our understanding of the metaphysical dimensions of light. When we comprehend light as a sacred object (especially in the form of fire), we see that it has a special value for the believer. However, light has also symbolic function: it points to the divine by analogy. God, Our Creator, is also Our Light and Our Warmth. The symbol itself can be sacred- therefore, *light can be a sacred symbol.*

3.5. Conclusion

The Divine light is not physical light. It cannot be produced mechanically in the way we light a fire. We, as human beings, do not have control over it. The Divine light is external to us, and all we can do is to accept its power.

We know that the Divine light exists from three different types of proofs: first, the biblical proof- the Divine light is mentioned and described in the Bible (also in the scene with Lord's Transfiguration); second, mystical experience point to its reality; and third, our intellect argues in favor of its existence: there is material (external), and there is inner (spiritual) light. Therefore, the latter could be associated with a divine source of light. The Divine light is also a symbol of God's power, might, and majesty.

Furthermore, the Divine light represents love and friendship. It helps us get closer to God. If we turn to the allegory created by Plato (the allegory of the cave), this light is like the sun which the prisoner can see after several years imprisonment in the cave. We need this light; we need the heat it produces. The Divine light is love; it is harmony, it makes us happy, it brings joy. This is a state which cannot be described but with metaphors and allegories. Paradoxes also should not be dismissed when we speak about God. Light and darkness sometimes co-exist in a strange connection which seems paradoxical. We will see some examples of this in the following chapter.

Chapter IV: The mysticism of light

Having discussed the nature and manifestations of the divine light, it is time now to turn back to our earthly experiences. We already stated that mystics claim that they have seen the Divine light. This sounds logical: mysticism relies on special techniques and methods which allow us to overcome the limitations of our body and perceptions. Especially by cleansing our soul, by adhering to good deeds, we can have more mystical experiences, including visions, encounters with supernatural beings, intellectual insights[23], and so forth. In what way are these experiences useful for us? Can we really have any benefits from them? What do we learn about God through them, and do they really prove His reality? These are some of the questions which will be subjected to analysis in the present chapter. To them, we will add another interesting topic: the connection between light and darkness.

4.1 The Divine darkness

Summary:

The conception of the Greek theologian Dionysius will be discussed here. He claims that the best method for gaining knowledge of God is the negative one- by not attributing to Him any quality. God stands above Being, above wisdom, above knowledge. This is what Dionysius calls Divine darkness- a superior reality which we can neither grasp nor understand.

---

[23] Of course, intellectual insights are not mystical in themselves. But sometimes mystical experiences can lead one precisely to such insights- for example, regarding the structure of the world, regarding the place of man in the world, etc.

It is logical to analyze the Divine darkness after the Divine light. But is there such "darkness"? It can sound absurd that there is "divine darkness" at all. The previous chapter dealt with the Divine light. God is light, as we postulated and proved; God radiates the light of truth, the light of the good, the light of life. Darkness is to be seen as evil, as death, as untruth. Where is the Divine darkness, then?

All this is true especially in the context of ethics and epistemology. When we refer to the essence of God, however, things change. *The conception of the Divine darkness is based on the idea that God stands beyond all of our concepts, notions, intuitions, feelings, experiences*, and so on. God's light is so bright that we cannot see it- because we do not have the senses for doing this. It is like those electromagnetic waves which we cannot perceive- the so-called infrared waves or ultraviolet waves. The length of the infrared waves exceeds our ability for perception; the length of the ultraviolet waves, on the other hand, stands below the threshold of our perception. This does not mean, still, that both types of waves do not exist. The very fact that we cannot perceive them does not deny their reality. God's light is to be understood in the same manner: it exceeds our abilities for perception, and we cannot perceive it. This is what is called Divine darkness- God's light is here, but we are not able to see it. Our inability to see a given entity can be called darkness- of course, metaphorically.[24]

Divine darkness, thus, can be defined as the *supraessential essence* of God (if we employ the conception of Gregory Palamas, which was already referred to). It stands

---

[24] Evidently, science cannot work with such a definition. Not seeing something is a defect. It can be called blindness, for instance. But in the case with God's light, we can say that blindness is an objective (not depending on us) state. We are naturally "blind" to the Divine light.

beyond anything we can understand, perceive, or feel. This is the principle of the apophatic (negative) theology, which was formulated for the first time in the works of the so-called Dionysius the Areopagite (5th century AD), whose real name has remained unknown. Dionysius divided theology into three types: positive, negative, and symbolic. The positive theology attributes only positive qualities to God- wisdom, truth, life, etc. The negative theology admits that these names can be attributed to God, but still rejects their absoluteness- they are only of relative nature. The symbolic theology can offer us only some metaphorical (and analogical) ways for grasping God's essence.

Before turning to the negative theology elaborated by Dionysius, it would be advisable to pay attention to the fact that this was not the first conception defining God in terms of negation. Similar ideas appeared in some Indian philosophical schools as well as in Taoism. One of the Buddhist schools claimed that the whole world is actually Nothing; this was the doctrine of emptiness (*sunyata*), elaborated by Nagarjuna in the 3rd century AD. Taoism in its classical form maintained that Being and Nothing, Truth and Untruth, Life and Death, coincide; that they are identical. Taoism (elaborated in the 5th century BC) stood close to the principle of dialectics, claiming that the opposites exist in unity. These two doctrines rejected any human ability to know the divine nature, even though they did not adhere to any belief in personal God. Here we should also add Ancient Jewish understanding of God as completely incognizable by humans. Ancient Jews felt great respect for the Lord and believed that people should not utter His name- a belief which has remained intact throughout the centuries. Still, the Old Testament offers some descriptions of God.

Here we will turn only to Taoism as an example of the conception that the opposites exist in unity, that light is darkness, that truth is untruth, and so forth. This principle was revealed in the book *Tao Te Ching*, whose author was most probably Lao Tzu. He writes there about *Tao* or the First principle of Being; although it is hard to translate what is *Tao* precisely. *Tao* is the Way, it is the Absolute, and also Being itself. In this short book, full of ambiguous passages, Lao Tzu advises his readers on political, moral, and ontological issues. Tao is described as unknown, as mysterious, as the only truth, and at the same time as the entity which cannot be grasped at all. At the same time, it can be grasped by *non-desiring* to know anything, by non-action, by pure passivity.

Tao escapes any definition: "The Tao is an empty vessel; it is used, but never filled" (Tao 4[25]). Tao is far from our understanding; to know Tao, means to get rid of one's own intellect, to not exercise one's intellectual powers at all. Tao is power, and still, it does not rule, as it is said in the book: "The world is ruled by letting things take their course. It cannot be ruled by interfering" (Tao 48). This phrase seems illogical, but the truth is that Lao Tzu does not teach complete passivity. What he wants to say here is that we will not know the essence of Tao by our own will; this can happen only if Tao reveals itself to us.

Furthermore, our intellect, our perceptions cannot be any source of knowledge of Tao. As Lao Tzu says: "Look, it cannot be seen - it is beyond Form" (Tao 14). It is an "empty vessel," hence it can take any form, and at the same time it is formless, it does not have any essence. We cannot define it neither as "light," nor as "dark": it is both, and it is neither of them: "From above it is not bright; From below it is not dark" (Tao 14). This is

---

[25] The number of the sections are referred to here.

a metaphor: the sky is usually associated with light (because of the sun), and the earth-with darkness (without sunlight it is dark). Lao Tzu indicates that both concepts can be interchangeable, and that the earth (or the entity which stands lower) can be identified with light, and the sky (or the entity which stands higher) can be associated with the dark. As it is written: "It returns to nothingness. The form of the formless, The image of the imageless" (Tao 14). Hence, it cannot be light, since light is something defined; and it is not darkness, for darkness is part of our common perception.

Tao is nothing itself; it does not exist in the usual sense of the term. It is in constant movement, and it is absolutely constant and immutable at the same time. This is because "the Tao is forever undefined. Small though it is in the unformed state, it cannot be grasped" (Tao 32). It is dark itself- for we cannot comprehend it: "Oh, it is dim and dark, and yet within is essence" (Tao 21). We cannot grasp its essence because Tao is constantly changing. How can one grasp the entity which never remains the same?

Such are some of the main postulates of Taoism, as we see. Still, the mystery hidden in this religious and philosophical doctrine is due also to the vagueness of the Chinese language itself. This cannot be said about Ancient Greek or Latin language. Hence, Dionysius could not use such vague phrases and sentences which can be interpreted in many ways at once. He tried to formulate a teaching, which would not define the divine essence strictly, but the language itself did not allow him to complete this task with absolute success. *Ergo*, he was forced to employ the method of dialectics.

We cannot be sure whether Dionysius was influenced by Taoism or the Buddhist doctrine of Nagarjuna. At any rate, the aforementioned Jewish tradition had a serious impact on Him. The mysticism typical of Orthodox theology is also to be considered a significant factor influencing Dionysius' work. Dionysius, in turn, was a great inspiration not only for Eastern (Orthodox) theologians but for Western ones as well.

In his reflections on the positive theology (in the book *On the Divine Names*), Dionysius refers to God as the Light. Here he explains why: "He fills every heavenly mind with spiritual light, and drives all ignorance and error from all souls where they have gained a lodgment, and giveth them all a share of holy light and purges their spiritual eyes from the mist of ignorance that surrounds them" (Dionysius, Divine names 94). The spiritual light is thus described as removing all errors and ignorance. This definition is epistemological: it reveals God as the truth, and the Divine light is the entity which radiates (disseminates) the Truth. Dionysius adds the following attributes to the Divine light: "And so that Good which is above all light is called a Spiritual Light because It is an Originating Beam and an Overflowing Radiance, illuminating with its fullness every Mind above the world, around it, or within it" (Dionysius, Divine names 94). God is the Good, and God is the light illuminating the minds of all human beings- not only their intellects but their souls as well.

Setting forth his negative theology, Dionysius emphasizes that God is endowed with all good attributes, but still, we cannot attribute them to Him- because He is beyond Being itself. As he observes: "We attribute lack of Reason to Him that is above Reason, and Imperfectibility to Him that is above and before Perfection; and Intangible and Invisible Darkness we attribute to that Light which is Unapproachable because It so far exceeds the visible light" (Dionysius, Divine names 150). The Divine light is Divine darkness at once; it is Light because it illuminates our soul, and it is darkness because we cannot grasp God in His very essence. To say it once again, *the Divine darkness is not evil; it is not deprivation or deficit. The Divine darkness indicates the limitations of the human mind and perceptions.* As created beings, we are not capable of grasping the nature of our Creator. This is what Dionysius means.

The method of dialectics used by the Greek theologian leads him to assert that *the knowledge and un-knowing of God are identical*: "Hence God is known in all things and apart from all things; and God is known through Knowledge and through Un-Knowing… He is All Things in all things and Nothing in any" (Dionysius, Divine names 152). God is beyond Being. Hence he does not exist- according to our common sense. Still, there should be some way to gain some knowledge of God, and Dionysius does not deny it. As he observes: "The Divinest Knowledge of God, the which is received through Unknowing, is obtained in that communion which transcends the mind, when the mind, turning away from all things and then leaving even itself behind, is united to the Dazzling Rays" (Dionysius, Divine names 152). It is easy to notice that Dionysius describes the state of contemplation here. Through contemplation, our mind will be able to grasp God's essence partially. The term "unknowing" should be comprehended as indicating that we have to forget about our earthly experience and knowledge, and look up to the skies (to the divine). Our knowledge about the world is relative, and we should not take it in an absolute sense. Contemplation will reveal to us what is the most important: the essence of God. Thanks to this, we will be able to understand what is the meaning of life. Our science cannot help us with finding this meaning.

There is no need to speak more about contemplation here; it has already been referred to in the present book. It is important to keep in mind the fact that contemplation is not a purely intellectual process. It requires "pure heart, "pure soul." That is, one should be cleansed from sins in order to see God's essence[26] (even partially). The act of contemplation comprises the whole human personality, not only one's soul, one's intellect, or one's spiritual side. The body is also actively engaged in this.

In another treatise, *The Mystical Theology*, the Greek author presents, in short, his conception about the Divine darkness and the negative way of theology. In the beginning of the treatise, Dionysius turns to the Holy Trinity and asks God to guide us to the realm which "exceedeth light and more than exceedeth knowledge, where the simple, absolute, and unchangeable mysteries of heavenly Truth lie hidden in the dazzling obscurity of the secret Silence, outshining all brilliance with the intensity of their darkness" (Dionysius, Mystical Theology 191). Therefore, the realm of the divine stands above knowledge- which means, above what we usually take as knowledge. The "secret Silence" is the knowledge of God, which is a kind of knowledge unattainable in the normal (logical, rational) way. The divine is a mystery, as the theologian postulates. For that reason, he calls this type of theology "mystical." It is mystical because it is not based on our ordinary understanding and daily experiences. This type of theology postulates that God is unknown and unknowable by the intellect. Its opposite is rational theology or the theological approach which is based on rational postulates.

A good example of rational theology is the teaching of Thomas Aquinas. Thomas elaborated his theology according to the principles of formal logic. Formal logic is held to be ineffective by mystics. According to them, formal logic helps us only in some situations- for example, when we want to calculate a certain amount of money, or when we try to gain more knowledge about the material world (especially, about the laws of

---

[26] We should not forget the fact that we cannot grasp God's essence on earth in its totality and completeness. Contemplation will help us to see only some aspects of it.

nature). Formal logic requires a strict definition of God in a positive way. For instance, a positive definition postulates that God is omniscient, powerful, omnipresent, wise, good, and so forth. However, if we say that God is not wise, because He stands beyond wisdom itself, then we have a rejection of formal logic. This rejection is clearly seen in the aforementioned book *Tao Te Ching*. Formal definitions are not of use in the realm of the divine, as mystics usually claim. The only source of true knowledge about God can, thus, be the personal encounter with Him in various mystical experiences. This is the ray Dionysius speaks about; this is the darkness which illuminates the world (as in the passage quoted above). As the Greek theologian puts it: "By the unceasing and absolute renunciation of thyself and all things, thou shalt in pureness cast all things aside, and be released from all, and so shalt be led upwards to the Ray of that divine Darkness which exceedeth all existence" (Dionysius, Mystical theology 191-2). The phrase "ray of divine Darkness" summarizes very well the basic principle of Dionysius' theology: that the Divine light is identical with darkness; that God is not only our sunshine but also the darkest night. Contrary to the conception of St. John of the Cross (who will be discussed in the third sub-chapter), the dark night is not full of fear and evil; it is rather a symbol of the divine mystery. As the Greek theologian assumes: "Unto this Darkness which is beyond Light we pray that we may come, and may attain unto vision through the loss of sight and knowledge, and that in ceasing thus to see or to know we may learn to know that which is beyond all perception and understanding" (Dionysius, Mystical theology 194).

The reader can be confused by reading the latter assertion. If Dionysius maintains that only negative theology is the proper way to the divine, then why should he admit that we can attain to God by contemplation? The "Darkness beyond Light" is a reality; it really exists. This is positive theology! The answer is simple: contemplation does not deny the power of negative theology. However, negative theology is not to be comprehended as an absolutely certain method. Negative theology should make us aware of our own limitations; of the fact that we cannot know absolutely everything about the world and its Creator; that whenever we think our knowledge is absolute and complete, we are in the wrong. Still, it is not typical for Christian theology and philosophy to prioritize the negative definitions of God over the positive ones. Negative theology fits perfectly in Taoism and Buddhism. They do not accept the idea of a personal God. Buddhism, for instance, claims that there are many forms of the divine, which can be called "gods"; but actually they are only manifestations of the divine. Moreover, the divine is not susceptible to any intellectual analysis; therefore, the use of the term "god" in Buddhism is provisional. In Taoism, it is the same.

The dialectical approach of Lao Tzu shows that the divine always escapes our attempts to define it precisely and permanently. Christian mentality, on the other hand, needs to have clear definitions of the divine. Even though the Eastern (Orthodox) Church seems more prone to the use of mystical methods and terminology, it is still based on the principles of rationalism (more precisely, formal logic) developed as early as in Ancient Greece. They can be seen in the works of Plato, Aristotle and the Stoics. Positive theology, thus, should not be dismissed. However, its knowledge of God must be based on contemplation; this, in some sense, goes beyond the principles of rationalism but it does not deny these principles. Formal logic can be employed, but it needs to be complemented with the mystical experiences of the contemplator.

As the reader can conclude, the Divine darkness, analyzed by Dionysius, is identical with the Divine light. Darkness here means the reality of God as standing beyond any understanding, feeling, experience. Still, this darkness is the brightest light, the most authentic reality. The paradox is present here; and still, Dionysius does not want to solve it.

Now, we can ask the question: Is the Divine light God Himself? Why should we take them as identical? In the previous chapter, we discussed the problem of the Tabor light. We discussed the theory of Palamas according to which this light represents the divine energies, and not God's essence itself. There is one conception claiming that the Divine light is not God. Let us turn to it now.

4.2 Van Ruysbroeck: The Divine light as an intermediary between God and man

Summary:

Here the teaching of the medieval mystic van Ruysbroeck will be discussed in short. His conception of the Divine light as an intermediary between God and humanity is quite interesting for us. It shows that the light itself is not God, but is necessarily connected with God. The Divine light is also associated with fire and flames by the mystic. Love is the way for grasping God's essence by means of contemplation.

An interesting mystic lived in the 14th century in Flanders. He was Jan van Ruysbroeck. Although not very popular, he can help us understand better the connection between God and the Divine light. What is remarkable in his conception is the assertion that the Divine light exists independently, as a medium between God and humanity.

Hence, the fact that we experience this light does not mean that we have encountered God's essence. His teaching is presented in manuscripts, some of which survived throughout the centuries, and was published in the 1860s under the title *The Book of the Twelve Beguines*. The book is mainly focused on the relationship God-man, on sin and evil, on righteousness and spirituality. Light is often associated with love, and the mystic often says that love is like fire. Part of the book is written in poetic form, thus making it possible for the reader to interpret it himself.

Van Ruysbroeck speaks about the love for God as helping us ascend to Him. You should have with you, the mystic says "a fiery Flame of devotion, leaping and ascending into the very Goodness of God Himself" (Ruysbroeck 68). To this, he also adds "a loving longing of the soul to be with God in His Eternity; a turning from all things of self into the freedom of the Will of God" (Ruysbroeck 68). The symbol of flame was already analyzed earlier in the present book. Fire here can be interpreted as life, as growth, as dynamics. A more important passage is found a bit further, where the author says that "The shining forth of That which hath no Mode is as a fair Mirror, wherein there shineth the Everlasting Light of God" (Ruysbroeck 69). However, this light itself is not God, as the mystic remarks: "It is not God; but it is that Light, Whereby we see Him" (Ruysbroeck 69).

What about the symbol of the Mirror? What is the Mirror? It is the shine of God, but it is not God itself. Like a mirror reflects a given object by producing an image, God produces light which we can see and enjoy. Thanks to this light, we are able to be with God, to know Him to some degree. This conception is very similar to the Palamas' teaching of the Tabor light and the energies of God. The light is "everlasting," which means that it is not of material essence. This light cannot be seen with our eyes; it is not an object of human perception. It should be rather understood as purely spiritual, as being present only to the contemplating soul. As van Ruysbroeck says: "They, who walk in the Divine Light thereof, discover in themselves the Unconfined" (Ruysbroeck 69).

Should this mean that the Light is an independent reality which exists in itself and *per se*? This is one of the questions which Barlaam formulated in his attempt to repudiate the conception of Palamas. By saying that the Divine light is not the essence of God, one gets closer to the assumption that the light itself is a god. Hence, there is another god besides the God of Christianity!

This assertion is not illogical. Still, it does not refer to the fact that the Divine light is independent but not from God. We perceive it separately because our own nature is limited. This light is the earthly manifestation of God, manifestation which is designed to be perceived by us (through our spiritual senses, as the theologians would say). This light is what we can encounter after an extended act of contemplation. We cannot encounter God Himself at once, in the very beginning of our contemplation. Many mystics have confirmed that it is the Divine light which appears first. It has many forms; it can be perceived in many ways. Some mystics feel awe; others feel joy. The third type of mystics are more reflective and try to understand what is going on and why. In all cases, there is light present in their visions. This is what van Ruysbroeck asserts: this Light helps us "see" (it is not normal perception) God in the proper way. In such a sense, the Divine light is the medium between God and us.

However, the Light itself is not a capsulated reality, existing completely independently from God. It is part of God, as Gregory Palamas writes: "If then the unapproachable is true and this light was unapproachable, the light was not a simulacrum of divinity, but truly the light of the true divinity, not only the divinity of the Son, but that of the Father and the Spirit too" (Palamas 74). Despite the fact that the Light should be discussed as a separate entity, it is still connected essentially with God, and with all Persons of the Holy Trinity. As Palamas puts it: "Therefore Christ possesses this light immutably, or rather, He has always possessed it, and always will have it with Him. But if it always was, is and will be" (Palamas 77). This statement means that the Divine light is eternal and unchangeable. It exists not only during the visions of the mystics; it has always been existing, completely objectively and independently from our mind and perception.

The following words by van Ruysbroeck may sound confusing, then. We stated that the light is independent of us. However, he says the following: "For It is the perfection of Nature, and above Nature, and is the clear-shining Intermediary between us and God. Our thoughts, bare and stripped of images, are themselves the Living Mirror wherein there shineth this Light" (Ruysbroeck 72). Should this mean that the Light would not exist without man? Is this light designed only for us, for human beings? Can it be grasped by other beings- for example, by angels? Without any doubt, the answer to the latter questions should be affirmative. Therefore, *the Divine light does not exist only for us; it is an objective reality*, but it is the only way for us to ascend to God spiritually (during our earthly existence, of course).

Contemplation is not only a result of cleansing our sins. It also results in cleansing our soul. Hence, this is a process which is dynamic and changing. Its effects are not less important than its goals. By contemplating the Divine light, one becomes really free, freed from one's earthly passions and desires: "Behold, therein appeareth a Light of the understanding, Which neither sense, nor reason, nor nature, nor the clearest logic can apprehend, but Which giveth us freedom and confidence towards God" (Ruysbroeck 71). Our soul becomes free not in the sense that it gains freedom of will (with which man is endowed from the very beginning). It becomes free because it is aware of the fact that there is a supreme reality, which stands beyond and above the world perceived by us in our daily living. This state of true freedom is accompanied by joy and happiness of the soul which can rejoice at being with God- although not completely. As the mystic remarks: "In this meeting of the Light with the stirring of God, is so great a joy and delight of the soul and body in his uplifted heart, that the man knoweth not what hath befallen him, nor how he may endure it" (Ruysbroeck 79-80). According to him, "this is called 'The Song of Joy,' which hath no words, and which no man knoweth, save him who hath conceived it in his heart" (Ruysbroeck 79-80). As we will see later, St. John of the Cross does not describe this encounter as a simple meeting. There are many stages in the act of contemplation of God, and not all of them bring real joy. The mystic Van Ruysbroeck emphasizes on the rejoice felt by the contemplator. This joy is not similar to our earthly feelings and emotions. It is such a state of joy which does not end; it cannot be exhausted. Unlike it, our earthly joy passes quickly, and it is often replaced by moments of sadness or indifference.

Another essential point to be emphasized is the fact that this mystical experience helps us understand our likeness to God and the fact that He is our Creator. We are the image of God, and this is clearly perceived thanks to the Divine light: "In this Living Mirror are we like to our Eternal Archetype, Which is God Himself; for we live a life conformable to the Everlasting Providence of God" (Ruysbroeck 72). This is the state of existence in which we can truly approach God. This happens thanks to the Divine light: *it makes the difference between our normal earthly existence and our state of being close to God*. During the act of contemplation, we not only attain to God; we can also become acquainted with ourselves, with our personality, with our (human) nature.

Van Ruysbroeck does not dismiss love in his works. Many mystics express their joy, which they often describe as true love. The contemplator's soul takes the Divine light through the means of love. As the mystic presents it: "There is thrown wide the Heaven which was shut, and from the Face of Divine Love there blazeth down a sudden Light, as it were a lightning-flash; and in that Light there speaketh the Spirit of Our Lord" (Ruysbroeck 79). The association of God with the beloved one is traditional for Christian theology. The very relation between God and man is often described (although metaphorically) as a romantic relationship, as love. God's love is immeasurable and cannot be exceeded by any other type of love: "The Love of God towards us is a stirring and purifying of the Spirit; whereby He distributeth His graces and His gifts to each several one of us, according to his need for the life of virtue" (Ruysbroeck 94). If the Divine light is the intermediary between God and us, love is the very relation between us and God. *By loving God, by loving the other human beings, by loving everything good, we are like God.* When our heart is open with and in love, God will call us and will show His love, as the mystic observes: "If thou hast thine heart alive, and open, and reverently uplifted unto God, the Light of His Grace will shine therein, will purify thy conscience, and will burn up all thy faults in the Fire of His Love" (Ruysbroeck 81). The fire of God's love is a metaphor which we already analyzed in the second chapter.

Love is so important, the mystic says, that it represents the final (fourth) stage[27] of the soul's ascending toward God. As van Ruysbroeck observes: "This Mode is called the uplifted and illuminated Exercise of love, according to the beloved Will of God. It is born of God together with the observances thereof" (Ruysbroeck 91). This is love which is illuminated, enlightened. The soul already knows the truth about the world, about God, and about humanity. This stage, however, will allow the soul to enjoy God's Love and Grace completely (as long as this is possible on earth, we have to remark). He adds that "This living soul, with true intention, with inward recollection, with forgetfulness and contempt of all that can impede or hinder it from the love of Our Lord, passeth on beyond itself" (Ruysbroeck 92-3). Man overcomes his limitations; he becomes a true image and likeness of God in this stage. The contemplator is now aware of the fact that God causes his joy, and only by God: "The enlightened intelligence and the will that is free go forward with thanks, and praise, and reverence, before the face of the Eternal Love" (Ruysbroeck 92-3). The phrase "Eternal love" here symbolizes God, and also the relation between God and humanity.

The works of van Ruysbroeck do not contain novel wisdom. They do not say anything novel (of course, in comparison with other prominent mystics). What they are remarkable for is the part played by the concepts of Light and Love. He demonstrates that both are interconnected and that *Love is the proper way to God*. Likewise other mystics (such as Hildegard von Bingen, St. Teresa of Avila, and others), van Ruysbroeck describes mystical experiences full of light. Light is everywhere, and the divine presence is ubiquitous; we only need to open our spiritual eyes and look up to the spiritual Heaven.

---

[27] The mystic presents the process of contemplation as having four stages, but they are not as precisely described as in St. John of the Cross.

We can see, then, God's traces everywhere around us. As the mystic puts it: "If thou standest in clear sunlight, turning thine eyes from all considerations of form and colour, and from all things whereon the sun shineth… thou wilt be led into that essence which is the sun itself" (Ruysbroeck 83). Moreover, the joy to become aware of this fact is more than anyone has experienced in our earthly life: "Thence cometh 'Joyfulness,' and the same is a heartfelt love, and a burning flame of devotion, for ever reverently turned to God in thankfulness and praise" (Ruysbroeck 80).

The conception of van Ruysbroeck about the Divine light is as simple as possible. It says that the Light is an intermediary between God and us; the Divine light itself cannot be God, although it is somehow radiated from God. As Dionysius claims, the Light and the Darkness of God could coincide; they could be even understood as the same entity. Hence, things are much more complicated. Mystical experiences are not based only on encounters with the Divine light. There is darkness; there is a long night experienced by some mystics. In order to know more about it, we will turn to one of the most prominent mystics in the history of Christianity.

4.3 St. John of the Cross: The Journey to God

Summary:

One of the most prominent mystics and theologians writes about several stages of the soul's ascending toward God. He explains how the soul passes through joy, pain, and sorrow, and joy again, and finally it becomes united with God. This conception shows how vital is mystical experience in the restoration of the initial relation between God and man.

The way to the Divine light is much more difficult than it can seem to the common man. Many people are prone to thinking that mystical experiences are easily accessible and that they bring only joy and happiness. St. John of the Cross, a Spanish mystic who lived in the 16th century, showed that this understanding is inadequate. Pain, suffering, confusion, tremor- all these feelings and emotions can accompany the journey of the mystic.

The theory of John of the Cross is presented in many of his works. The most famous of these is *The Dark Night of the Soul*. Here we will refer to other two of his works: *Spiritual Canticle between the Soul and Christ*, and *The Living Flame of Love*. These two books comprise the same issues which are analyzed in *The Dark Night of the Soul* but are written in a simpler manner. The method used by the Spanish theologian is to present his poems devoted on God, and then to interpret them analytically. This allows for diverse interpretations, thanks to the symbols employed in the poems.

The basis of the conception of St. John is his idea that the mystical journey to God has four stages. One passes through initial joy, then one encounters darkness, and finally one becomes one with God. God is understood as the Light, but the encounter with Him can also lead to a feeling of Darkness, as we will see further. Darkness is comprehended in two ways: first, as the absence of light (and thus, as the realm of the evil power); and second, as the sphere in which our senses and intellect do not work properly.

In the first stanza dealing with the problem of light (Stanza X) light is contrasted to darkness. As St. John says: "Let my eyes behold Thee Who art- their light, and it is for

Thee alone I would use them.[28]" This stanza is explained by the theologian in the following manner: "God is the supernatural light of the soul; without which it abides in darkness. And now, in the excess of its affection, it calls Him the light of its eyes, after the manner of earthly lovers when they would exhibit the affection they bear to the object of their love" (John of the Cross 53). It is important to note that God is associated with Light in all works of St. John. Notwithstanding, He is perceived as darkness by us (for the reasons which we already elucidated when we discussed Dionysius). St. John observes that "The soul by a certain fitness deserves the Divine light, if it shuts its eyes against all objects whatever, and opens them only for the Vision of God" (John of the Cross 54). This is the act of contemplation. How does this act begin? What is necessary for it to take place? The initial stage is called by St. John *ecstasy*. This is completely logical: many philosophers call it that way. Plotinus, a Neoplatonic philosopher, described quite well the process of ecstasy. According to Plotinus, this is a stage when the soul goes out of the body (metaphorically said), and thus it goes beyond all limitations imposed by the material world. The very word has its origin in Ancient Greek- *extasis* means to go beyond oneself. The word was then borrowed in Latin, and later in English. The difference between the conception of Plotinus and the teaching of St. John of the Cross is that Plotinus denied any function, any part of the body during this process. Plotinus expressed his disgust to the body and anything material. This is not a view which could be endorsed by Christian theologians. The contemplator is one whole- a union of body and soul. For Plotinus (and other Neoplatonists), this could not be the

---

[28] These are only extractions from the stanzas. The reader should read the stanzas himself to form an opinion about them.

case- precisely this is the basis of the conception of *extasis*[29]. Plotinus held that *extasis* is the only way to attain to the Supreme Entity, to The One. The One is the source of all Being and life. It is of ideal nature; therefore, one can attain to it only spiritually. St. John has another opinion on the issue: the body is not to be scorned, but still, it does not have a significant part in the process. Still, St. John prefers using the word "soul," which we should interpret rather as "person," or the believer himself[30].

The process of one's attaining to God is described in Stanza XIII which says: "The wounded hart looms on the hill in the air of thy flight and is refreshed." This is interpreted by the theologian as follows: "The spirit of man, in this visitation of the Spirit of God, is rapt upwards in Divine communion; the body is abandoned, all its acts and feelings are suspended, because the soul is absorbed in God" (John of the Cross 70). This stage is initiated by the Holy Spirit, not by the contemplator himself. We need the help of the Holy Spirit to enter the act of contemplation. The body is "abandoned" in the sense that its needs and desires are no longer important. The soul is "absorbed in God" not because it has already achieved the unity with and in God, but since the soul is amazed by the process taking place. It is one's first true encounter with God.

Speaking about the process of one's attaining to God, the reader may object that St. John of the Cross uses too freely the concepts of ecstasy and contemplation. It is not clear how this process can be named in general. Is it contemplation? Is it merely an ecstasy? Is it a series of visions? As a matter of fact, the process can be called contemplation; however, it contains also visions, encounters with God and angels, talks

---

[29] Here we refer to the Greek word used by Plotinus.
[30] The medieval Christian tradition adhered to using the word "soul" instead of "man." Still, we can say that both were used in identical sense.

with saints, as well as the spiritual state called ecstasy. The very word "process" is not the most appropriate, for it indicates that every contemplator feels and experiences absolutely the same. For that reason, we can employ various names and descriptions, which convey all these meanings and associations.

Now, let us examine contemplation further. Referring to Stanza XIII, St. John elucidates the nature of contemplation: "Contemplation is lofty eminence where God, in this life, begins to communicate Himself to the soul, and to show Himself, but not distinctly" (John of the Cross 71). He adds that this knowledge is limited: "It is said, 'Looms on the hill,' because he does not appear clearly. However profound the knowledge of Himself which God may grant to the soul in this life, it is, after all, but an indistinct vision" (John of the Cross 71). The soul is refreshed since it has some knowledge about God and now feels joy. But it needs something more in order to continue ascending toward God: love. As St. John puts it: "Notwithstanding the highest knowledge of God, and contemplation itself, together with the knowledge of all mysteries, the soul without love is nothing worth, and can do nothing, as the Apostle saith, towards its union with God" (John of the Cross 72). As it was mentioned in the previous sub-chapter, love is necessary for the soul eager to be united with God. Love, however, does not appear from nothing. It has to be the result of one's good will. *We have to have real intentions to be united with God and to love God. We should not do it only out of curiosity*, for instance. The true believer should not boast with his mystical experiences, with the fact that he has seen the Divine light. Love should be the basis of contemplation, and love does not accept boasting. When one loves, one is modest. It is not by accidence that St. John compares the soul with a bride and God with the bridegroom. Their relationship is similar to that of two young people in love. But this is love of the highest type, love full of spiritual insights, hope, compassion. It is far from egoistic love, from a relationship in which both persons tend to insists on their own ambitions and desires. This relationship is made real by God Himself, and it is only Him Who can end it. The soul must be willing to enter the relationship, as St. John confirms: "God does not establish His grace and love in the soul but in proportion to the good will of that soul's love. He, therefore, that will love God must strive to love Him more and more, that his love fail not" (John of the Cross 73).

St. John goes on further in his presentation of the journey of the soul. Stanza XIV compares God to mountains and valleys, to "the strange islands, the roaring torrents, the whisper of the amorous gales." This stanza means, the theologian writes, that God stands too far from us, and we can never attain to Him completely: "We are not to think that what the soul perceives, though pure truth, can be the perfect and clear fruition of Heaven. For though it be free from accidents, it is not clear, but rather obscure, because it is contemplation" (St. John of Cross 82). He adds that "we may say that it is a ray and an image of fruition because it occurs in the intellect, the seat of fruition" (John of the Cross 82). With these words, the author prepares the reader for introducing another important concept- the Dark and/or Tranquil night. As it is written in Stanza XV: "The tranquil night at the approaches of the dawn, the silent music, the murmuring solitude, the supper which revives, and enkindles love." This is one of the most prominent ideas of St. John of the Cross. The night is the condition in which the soul no longer adheres to the thoughts, feelings, and experiences related to its earthly life. The senses and the intellect are in the dark now. However, this night is tranquil- it does not terrify the soul. This state is interpreted as follows: "In this spiritual sleep in the bosom of the Beloved the soul enters into the possession and fruition of all the calmness, repose, and quiet of a peaceful night, and receives at the same time in God a certain unfathomable obscure Divine intelligence" (John of the Cross 85). Dionysius would say something similar- that this is the Divine darkness or Light which exceeds our perception and intellect. Still, St. John distinguishes between two types of Night (darkness); the Obscure night, and the Tranquil night. The obscure night is the state when one feels completely disoriented and confused. On the other hand, "This tranquil night is not like a night of obscurity, but rather like the night when the sunrise is drawing nigh" (John of the Cross 85). He goes on: "This tranquillity and repose in God is not all darkness to the soul, as the Obscure Night, but rather tranquillity and repose in the Divine light and in the new knowledge of God, whereby the mind, most sweetly tranquil, is elevated upwards to Divine light" (John of the Cross 85). Hence, it can be interpreted as a transition between the Obscure night and the Tranquil night. Here the mind (the soul) feels calm; there is no more amazement, awe, or joy. All these feelings have passed, and the soul is prepared to ascend higher. The soul is seemingly left alone, with itself. It can reflect now on its experiences and feelings. This state is compared to twilight: "It is then neither wholly night nor wholly day, but twilight, so this solitude and Divine repose is neither perfectly illuminated by the Divine light, not yet perfectly alien from it" (John of the Cross 85). It is not a real night, then. We can say that it is the transition from a Night to a Day. There is some light there; and still, this light is not enough to fill the soul with joy. As St. John puts it: "It is like a man who after a profound sleep opens his eyes to unexpected light" (John of the Cross 85).

The reader can say that this stage is not necessary. Why the contemplator needs to pass through such "tranquil night"? Does it make any difference to his knowledge and experience? Perhaps St. John is eager to demonstrate that there should be some transition between the Day and the Night; that the Divine light and the Divine darkness are not absolutely the same. Dionysius would assert that their identity is dialectical. St. John does not accept such a dialectical approach: each stage of the process of attaining to God has its internal logic. From initial illumination (produced by the Holy Spirit), one passes through the Day (by contemplating the Divine light). Next, he passes through the night, which has two stages: the first one is the state of disorientation and ignorance, and the second one is the state when the soul is alone and is preparing itself to go higher. There is logic in this hierarchy. Furthermore, the state of "tranquil night" provides the soul with some knowledge: "In this silence and tranquillity of the night, and in this knowledge of the Divine light, the soul discerns a marvellous arrangement and disposition of God's wisdom in the diversities of His creatures and operations" (John of the Cross 86). *Ergo*, the soul does not look only in itself; it also takes a look around, trying to understand the nature of the Creation. St. John goes on: "In the same way, in this tranquil contemplation, the soul beholds all creatures, not only the highest, but the lowest also, each one according to the gift of God to it, sending forth the voice of its witness to what God is" (John of the Cross 87). This means the soul is still not completely acquainted with the nature of God. It begins feeling love for God, by seeing how much He has done, and how much He cares about us and all other creatures. Not that this is the first moment when the soul feels love for God; but it is the moment when this love becomes endless. The soul knows now that it owes its existence to God. It realizes how big is the Grace of God, and how much has it received from God. As St. John explains it: "The Beloved is Himself the supper which revives, and enkindles love, refreshing the soul with His abundance, and enkindling its love in His graciousness" (John of the Cross 89).

The love of the bride (the soul) for God (the Beloved) leads to their union. The initial good relation between God and man is restored. This is described in Stanza XXXIX where the author says: "The song of the sweet nightingale… In the serene night, with the fire that consumes but without pain." This is the final stage of the soul's ascending to God. As St. John observes: "This is to show the entire perfection of that love, for these two qualities are necessary to constitute its perfection" (John of the Cross 209). The soul will be transformed ("consumed" by the "fire") and will partake in God from then on: "It must consume the soul, and transform it in God: this burning and transformation also must be painless. Now this can never happen except in the state of bliss, and where this fire is sweet love" (John of the Cross 209). The pain and sorrow are already in the past. The ultimate restoration is achieved. There is no anything more to want and to strive for.

Another short work by St. John- *The Living Flame of Love*- is focused on the relation God-man. This relation is symbolized by the Flame of Love. Three words here are important to note: living, flame, and love. St. John wants to show the reader that only by love can we attain to God. The flame here indicates the Eternal source of all life, of all existence, of all creation. As St. John of the Cross observes: "This flame of love is the Spirit of the Bridegroom, the Holy Ghost, of whose presence within itself the soul is conscious" (John of the Cross 220). The term "living" refers to God's eternity, to the fact that He stands beyond any death and decay. As St. John explains: "This is the reason why this Flame is said to be a living flame, not because it is not always living, but because its effect is to make the soul live spiritually in God" (John of the Cross 222). Life in the usual sense is only part of our earthly existence. There is another type of Life- the Eternal reality, the reality which stands beyond our normal being. The Living Flame is what makes us immortal; it guarantees our immortality.

Immortality is the notion which cannot be dismissed while speaking about God. Once attained to God, the soul knows already that it will last forever, that it will never cease to exist. In spite of this, man and God are not equally immortal, if we can say it that way. God is not immortal, for He does not need to be so- He cannot be subjected to death. The Living Flame of Love, therefore, is Eternal; and we can enjoy our immortality in It.

Love itself is the method and the nature of our union with God. As St. John points out, "Love unites the soul with God, and the greater its love the Degree- of love for God, deeper does it enter into God, and the more is it centred in Him" (John of the Cross 225). He adds further: "We may say, that as the degrees of love, so are the centres, which the soul finds in God. These are the many mansions of the Father's house" (John of the Cross 225). The more we love God, the more are the centers which the soul inhabits in God. This means, its knowledge and experience of being with God increases. This is a gradual process, which is endless and cannot cease. Once started loving God, the soul will continue doing it for all eternity.

One of the forms of Divine love is Light, as the Spanish mystic remarks: "God, Who seeks to enter the soul by union and the transformation of love, is He who previously enveloped the soul, purifying it with the light and heat of His Divine Flame, which was before grievous but is now sweet" (John of the Cross 227). God's Light is purifying; it warms the soul, meaning that the soul feels loved. The process of the soul's attaining to God is finished now, and the pain has been transformed into sweetness, into joy. The soul can rejoice to be together with God, with the angels, with the saints, and with all other righteous people in Heaven. The true Light of God is now near the soul, and the soul knows already everything needed about the world, about God, and about the creatures.

It is now time for the soul to thank God. All this has been achieved thanks to the Power and Mercy of God. The soul is aware of that, and it wants to express its gratitude. This is described in one of the stanzas- Stanza III, part of which reads as follows: "The deep caverns of sense, obscure and dark, with unwonted brightness give light and heat together to the Beloved." As St. John goes on: "The bride-soul from her inmost heart gives thanks to the Bridegroom for the great mercies which, in the state of union, she has received at His hands, for He has bestowed upon her therein a manifold and most profound knowledge of Himself" (John of the Cross 253). The bride has passed the long way to her Beloved, and their union will last forever. The Eternal Flame of Love will shine forever: "These powers, previous to the state of union, were in darkness and obscurity, but are now illuminated by the fires of love and respond thereto, offering that very light and love to Him who has kindled and inspired them" (John of the Cross 253). The journey is a happy one: the soul is now married to her Beloved.

The teaching of St. John of the Cross should not be taken literally. It contains plenty of symbols which can be subjected to various interpretations. One of the examples is the symbol of night- it can be associated with lack of knowledge, with tranquility, with self-reflection, and others. St. John helps his readers understand all these stages of the soul's journey to God. His optimistic attitude has assisted many believers to be aware of the fact that sorrow and pain are an inevitable part of such a journey, but in the end, they are always replaced by real joy.

The initial relation God-man will be restored, St. John is convinced. We have to believe in this, and still, we must take action to achieve it, as long as this is in our hands. Instead of being proud and egocentric, we have to realize that only love can help us ascend to God. Love- an abstract word, much more abstract than all the meanings of light. Love- a word which is often abused and misinterpreted. Love- one of the basic values of Christianity. Love is part of the Divine light; love is a symbol, and at the same time- an exemplification of this Light. There is no way leading to God but the Way of Love. Love has many forms, this is true. Still, the fact that some people associate love only with romantic relationship show how wrong they are. *True love does not have individual form, it goes across and beyond any limitations and borders. It is love which aims at doing good, helping, caring, improving, purifying*, and so forth. The Eternal Flame of Love is pure, good, and bright.

4.4 Conclusion

There are many Christian mystics describing the presence of the Divine light in their life, or in some situations. The present book does not refer to St. Teresa of Avila, to Hildegard von Bingen, to John Bunyan, and others. It has to be remarked, still, that the mystical experience is diverse and it cannot be generalized in one chapter. At any rate, the mystical experience helps in three ways:

1. It helps the believer to find God and to return to God.

2. It provides the believer with the necessary knowledge to grasp God's essence.

3. It provides the believer with the answer to the question regarding the meaning of life.

The third of these points should not be ignored. Our time has brought the sense of apathy, of indifference toward man's existence. It is often said that our life does not have any objective sense; that we can "create" our own meaning and adhere to it. Mystical experience, especially of Christian mystics, demonstrate the opposite- that life has objective meaning. The latter is found in God, and in our relation with God. God brings the Light to our life; God is our Sun; thanks to God we can live, breathe, feel, love, think, believe, pray. But God is not merely the Light; He is all possible forms of Light, among them being even Divine darkness. Dialectically said, Light and Darkness coincide in God. God's Light is dark, and God's Darkness is bright. The basis of this teaching (elaborated by Dionysius) is the assumption that we can never grasp God's essence, and that He stands beyond all our concepts, perceptions, and thoughts. Hence, we can experience the divine both as light and as darkness. Still, St. John of the Cross shows that there is some difference between them and that it is better to use formal logic while describing the journey of the soul to God. *Light is the condition of the soul united with God.* There is no brighter and truer Light than this.

Conclusion

The current book presents only some dimensions of the notion of light. As we said in the beginning, we do not deal with the scientific concept of light. At any rate, contemporary Physics has reached several interesting facts regarding light- first, that it has limited speed; second, that it consists of particles which behave also as waves; and third, that light travels for some time from the sun and other astronomical objects- therefore, we do not see the stars as they are right now, but rather as they were some moments ago. Thus, the material aspects of light are not less interesting than its metaphysical connotations. However, this should be the topic of another book.

Metaphysically, light has been seen by the philosophers as one of the fundamental principles of life, and also of Being. Without light, life would be impossible to take place, it is asserted- and not without arguments. Light helps us orientate in the world; we can do all our daily activities thanks to light and lighting. Light provides us with warmth, especially in the form of fire. Light provokes feelings and emotions. Light is romantic; light is melancholic; and so forth. Light has many meanings, connotations, associations. What is universal about the metaphysical understanding of light is its positive power. Light is always seen as good, as having a positive impact on our world, on man, on the animal realm, etc.

Then we turn to the ethical side of light. In many religions, the supreme divinities are seen as shining bright, as associated with fire and/or light. A good example of this is Mithra, the sun-god, which we analyzed in the first chapter. It was shown also that many nations have traditions related to the summer solstice- a celebration which aims to demonstrate that sunlight affects fertility, life, health, the well-being of people. Light is good; darkness is evil, then.

The potential of darkness, or the dark side of our nature, was analyzed by Carl Gustav Jung. According to him, we can compare our consciousness with light, and our unconscious with darkness. All our instincts, unconscious desires, etc., are located "under the surface." But we should not take them as entirely negative. On the contrary: both parts of our *psyche* must work with each other. There should be harmony between them, in the ideal state of affairs. This is demonstrated in Jung's theory of the Shadow.

The idea that light and darkness can coincide, and that they could even interact with each other, was elaborated in the fourth chapter. The Taoist understanding of light as identical with darkness stands close to the mystical theologian Dionysius, who claims that God radiates darkness, and not light- for, we can never grasp His true nature. Hence, when we speak about Divine light, this is only an analogy.

Still, the discussion on the nature of the Tabor light, which was presented in the third chapter, is good evidence in favor of the theory that God's Light (the Divine light) can be experienced on earth. Even though this does not seem logical, it can happen, some Byzantine theologians claim. This is not light which can be seen with our eyes; only our spiritual senses can "see" it. This conception can help us understand the mystical experiences described in the fourth chapter. If we cannot experience the Divine light on earth, what is the light seen by the mystics, then? As it turns out, the Divine light can be understood as an intermediary between God and man, as the medieval mystic van Ruysbroeck asserts.

One final remark is needed. The Divine light should not be understood entirely in terms of mysticism. Not everyone can have real mystical experiences. And the fact that a certain person does not have such does not mean that the person is deprived of God's Grace. Our love for God, our gratitude, our compassion to all human beings, our faith in

God- all this can be symbolized by God's light. If we have love, we have the Light within

us.

Works cited

The Bible. *New International Version*. Print.

Bachelard, Gaston. *The Psychoanalysis of Fire*. London: Routledge & Kegan Paul, 1964.

Print.

Catechism of the Catholic Church. Web.

<http://www.vatican.va/archive/ENG0015/_INDEX.HTM>

Cumont, Franz. *The Mysteries of Mithra*. Chicago: The Open Court Publishing Company;

London: Kegan Paul, Trench, Trübner & Co, 1903. Print.

Dionysius the Areopagite. "The Divine Names." *On the Divine Names. Mystical*

Theology, New York: Macmillan, 1920, pp. 50-190. Print.

Dionysius the Areopagite. "The Mystical Theology." *On the Divine Names. Mystical*

Theology, New York: Macmillan, 1920, pp. 191-201. Print.

Diwali Festival. Meaning and Significance. Web.

<http://www.diwalifestival.org/diwali-meaning-significance.html>

Eduljee, K. E. Fire and Light. *Zoroastrian Heritage*. Web.

<http://www.heritageinstitute.com/zoroastrianism/worship/fire.htm>

Eliade, Mircea. *The Sacred and the Profane*. New York: Harcourt, Brace & World, Inc.,

1963. Print.

Feshbach, Sidney. "The Light at the End of the Tunnel is Coming Right at Me, or, the

Dialectic of Elemental Light and Elemental Dark." *The Elemental Dialectic of*

Light and Darkness, edited by Anna-Teresa Tyminiecka, Springer, 1992, pp. 55-

84. Print.

Fox, Douglas. "Darkness and Light: The Zoroastrian View." *Journal of the American*

Academy of Religion, vol. 35, no. 2, 1967, pp. 129-137. Print.

Frazer, James. *The Golden Bough*. Temple of Earth Publishing. N.d. Web.

<http://www.templeofearth.com/books/goldenbough.pdf>

Garrigou-Lagrange, Reginald. *Life Everlasting*. N.P. N. D. Web.

   <http://www.documenta-

   catholica.eu/d_Garrigou%20-%20Lagrange,%20R%20-%20Life%20Everlasting

   %20-%20EN.pdf>

St. John of the Cross. *Complete Works*, vol. II. London: Longman, Green, 1864. Print.

Jung, Carl. *Aion*. Collected Works, edited by Herbert Read et al., vol. 9, part II. Princeton

   University Press, 1968. Print.

Krishna, Vamshi. The Psychology of Fear of the Dark. Web.

   <http://yourdost.com/blog/2016/03/the-psychology-of-fear-of-the-dark.html>

Meyendorf, John. "Mount Athos in the Fourteenth Century: Spiritual and Intellectual

   Legacy". *Dumbarton Oaks Papers,* vol. 42, 1988, pp. 157-165. Print.

Palamas, Gregory. *The Triads*. Paulist Press, 1983. Print.

Religion Facts. Light and Darkness (Primitive). Web.

   <http://www.religionfacts.com/library/encyclopedia-religion-ethics/light-

   darkness-primitive>

Van Ruysbroeck, Jan. *The Book of the Twelve Beguines*. London: John Watkins, 1913.

Ryba, Thomas. "Elemental Forms, Creativity and the Transformative Power of Literature

   in A.-T. Tymieniecka's *Tractatus Brevis*." *The Elemental Dialectic of Light and

   Darkness*, edited by Anna-Teresa Tyminiecka, Springer, 1992, pp. 3-26. Print.

Sanna, Emily. Why Do Christians Use Incense? Web.

<http://www.uscatholic.org/articles/201508/why-do-christians-use-incense-30320>

Tao Te Ching. Translated by Gia Fu Feng, Jane English. N.d., n.p. Web.

<http://www.dankalia.com/more/taoteching.pdf>

Tomassoni, Rosella; Galetta, Giuseppe; Treglia, Eugenia. "Psychology of Light: How Light Influences the Health and Psyche." *Psychology*, vol. 6, 2015, pp. 1216-1222.

<http://dx.doi.org/10.4236/psych.2015.610119>

Tselengidis, Dimitrios. *The Contribution of St. Gregory Palamas to Hesychasm. Theological Pressupositions of the Life in the Holy Spirit*. Web.

<http://www.saintnicodemos.org/documents/Final_Tselengides_Word.pdf>

Tymieniecka "The Theme." *The Elemental Dialectic of Light and Darkness,* edited by Anna-Teresa Tyminiecka, Springer, 1992, pp. VII-VIII. Print.

Ventegodt, Søren; Andersen, Niels; Merrick, Joav. "The Life Mission Theory v. Theory of the Anti-Self (the Shadow) or the Evil Side of Man". *The Scientific World Journal,* vol. 3, 2003, pp. 1302-1313. Web.

<DOI 10.1100/tsw.2003.117>

Whitman, Walt. *O Sun of Real Peace*. Web.

<http://whitmanarchive.org/published/LG/1871/poems/168>

Williams, Steven. "The Transfiguration of Jesus Christ." *Themelios*, vol. 28, no. 1, 2002, pp. 13-25. Print.